BIG ZUU'S
BIG EATS

BIG ZUU'S BIG EATS

"No pressure, just food pleasure"

BOOKS

BBC Books, an imprint of Ebury Publishing
20 Vauxhall Bridge Road,
London SW1V 2SA

BBC Books is part of the Penguin Random House group of companies whose addresses
can be found at global.penguinrandomhouse.com

Copyright © UKTV Media & Boom 2021
Food and cover photography © Ellis Parrinder 2021
Series photography © UKTV Media 2021

Big Zuu has asserted his right to be identified as the author of this Work in accordance
with the Copyright, Designs and Patents Act 1988

This book is published to accompany the television series entitled *Big Zuu's Big Eats* first
broadcast on Dave in 2020. *Big Zuu's Big Eats* is a Boom and UKTV Media production.

Executive Producers: Sam Grace and Natalie Rose
Series Director: Chris Faith
Series Producer: Alex Gilman

First published by BBC Books in 2021

www.penguin.co.uk

A CIP catalogue record for this book is available from the British Library

ISBN 9781785947292

Publishing Director: Albert DePetrillo
Project Editor: Nell Warner
Design: Louise Evans
Food photography: Ellis Parrinder
Series photography: Rob Youngson
Food Stylist and Home Economist: Rosie Mackean
Food Stylist's Assistant: Sonali Shah
Prop Stylist: Alexander Breeze
Contributing Writer: Alex Gilman
Copy Editor: Jane Birch
Production: Catherine Ngwong

Printed and bound by C&C Offset Printing Ltd, China

Penguin Random House is committed to a sustainable future for our business, our readers
and our planet. This book is made from Forest Stewardship Council® certified paper.

INTRODUCTION

My first time making a roux, Food Technology (2008). Combine the butter and flour. I melted the butter, added the flour and couldn't believe the golden concentration that was created before my 13-year-old eyes. When I added milk to the roux, I suddenly realised that my first sauce was being created. Questions like 'Am I a chef?', 'Am I better than my mum at cooking?' and 'Did we learn about this in science?' all came into my mind. Once I had finished gradually adding the milk and seasoned it with white pepper ('cause apparently that looks nicer), my teacher handed me a block of cheese. I integrated this and layered the sauce over boiled pasta, smothered more grated cheese over it, put it in the oven and that was my first-ever macaroni cheese. Since then, I've had so much mac 'n' cheese I'm lactose intolerant, but I am still The Roux Lord. That was also my first experience of cooking in an actual kitchen. Before that, I was in my little house on Fernhead Road warming up macaroni cheese from a can, from Lidl, in a microwave.

Years later, I still loved food (if you couldn't tell by my big appearance), but music captured my heart, so I left university after studying youth work, to become a Grime MC. My personality was something that was connected to my music, meaning food increasingly became part of my identity. This love was made even more apparent when I did a cooking video online that summoned The Roux Lord, making another macaroni cheese, leading to a production company hollering at man to create what is now *Big Zuu's Big Eats*.

So thank you macaroni cheese, St Augustine's, Lidl, DFR and Taz for filming that video. Thank you Boom, TwoFour and UKTV for making *Big Eats*, thank you BBC Books for adding to this wavy journey of expression through food – proof that anyone from anywhere can be a TV chef and sell some books... or two. Thank you to all the fans and supporters who have always been behind us and given us a platform to show diverse views on food, like being able to share my West African roots or Tubsey and Hyder getting to celebrate their interpretation of Iraqi and Kurdish cooking. Thank you.

For all the people who ask me for recipes, I'm now just going to tell you to read the book, so you have no excuse not to get cheffy with it. But, if you are a new reader and you've just got this as a random present, hopefully you can use these recipes to create some different types of food that you may have never tasted or heard of before, brought to you by a roadman and the two bredrins he went to school with.

This year has been a mad one, but the energy that has gone into this book is so wholesome and deep-rooted into my life that I'm hoping this can make a change within your home and open your eyes to international flavours, with a story confirming its authenticity, plus some slang that you may not understand. Just ask your niece or nephew if you need some assistance though and they'll also think you're cool for having a Big Zuu book.

MUMMA ZUU

The woman I owe it all to. You gave me life. The opportunity to be the person I am.

My mum left Sierra Leone in 1995 because of the rebel war happening in her country and found refuge in England when she was 26 years old and four months pregnant with her first son (me) – 25 years later I'm talking about her journey and sharing her recipes with you in a cookbook. The world is bizarre, but it's made the strongest person I've ever seen, my mother, Miss Isatu Hamzie.

She was called 'Mummy' by everyone, even by her late father, which confused me because my grandad was calling my mum 'Mummy', haha, but it meant she was the mother of the family. As one of the oldest of 14 siblings, she was cooking from a young age, so her experiences are so deep that she could tell you stories for days about her journey with food growing up in a place like Sierra Leone. It was, and still is, deep in poverty yet rich in produce that I wish we could have access to over here. Funny how life works.

My mum was pregnant with my little brother Feroz in 2006 and by the end of her pregnancy she was incredibly fatigued a lot of the time, which is understandable when you are carrying a life inside of you. I wanted to help, so I started to cook dinner because I knew it would ease some of the strain off her.

A dish I remember making at the time, aged ten, was tortellini with tomato sauce, which my mum used to boil like dried pasta, for ten minutes! It would always come out soggy, haha, because she didn't realise the difference in it being fresh pasta and as Africans we love making sure stuff is cooked LOOL. I read the Sainsbury's packet and it said 'boil for 2–3 minutes', so that's exactly what I did. When I served my mum this al dente pasta with a lil' seasoned tomato sauce, she couldn't believe that her little son just schooled her on how to chef a fresh pasta dish. She was so proud that I took initiative as a little man in our house to ease this pressure and also made her a nice dinner in the process, which then turned into a nice breakfast, lunch and so forth.

Looking back, our journey with food has been emotional – from me wanting more westernised dishes at home and less jollof rice, to now begging her for fufu and okra soup every week.

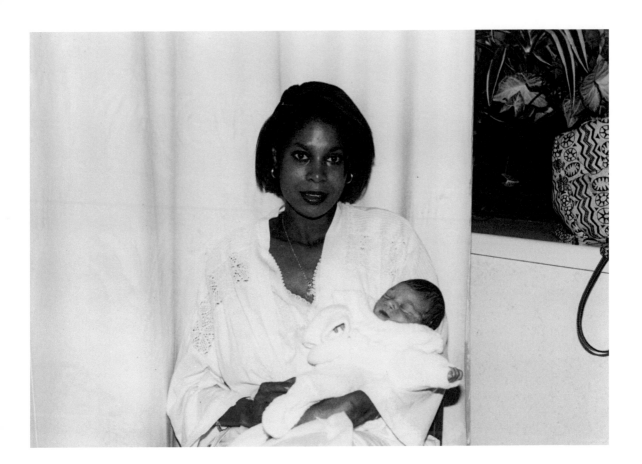

‘We really do balance out each other in the kitchen, whether it’s me showing her how to make fajitas properly or her showing me how to prepare cassava leaf for a stew.’

I hope you can learn more about my mum’s culture and background through her recipes and also pick up some dishes from her son, who’s used all that knowledge from first cooking that pasta for her, aged ten.

I love you Mum and I’m proud that we are able to share your passion for food with the world and also prove that all those years of cooking for others and the sacrifices you’ve made for me and my brother were all worth it.

xxx

ZUU, TUBSEY & HYDER

What do you get when you put a mixed-race rapper, an Iraqi delivery mogul and a retired semi-pro Kurdish international footballer with nothing but three GCSEs in Food Tech and six months on the grills in Nando's together? A primetime television cooking show.

Zuhair, Ahmed and Hyder (aka Zuu, Tubsey and Hyder) are lifelong friends from Harrow Road who went to secondary school together and are now embarking on a culinary journey in a revamped food world. There is a flock of fresh, hungry food-content creators that is moving so mad that my brudda Gordon Ramsay now has a TikTok account.

The lads have always loved cooking with each other, ever since they whipped up their first roux in Food Tech with Miss Johnson. Thanks to her, the *Big Zuu's Big Eats* food truck has maintained its 5-star hygiene rating, especially after she enlightened them on the dangers of staphylococcus aureus (we'll let you look that one up on your own). From there, real life crept in and they went down their separate paths of adulthood, but still remained brothers.

Zuu somehow became a rapper (even though Tubsey was spitting bars well before him) and, alongside his journey to becoming a musical sensation, he ventured into the food world. Through the power of social media, he was offered a television programme to cook with comedians. The original intention was to have Zuu alongside other 'food influencers' but the producers couldn't find the right fit for Zuu's cooking accomplices – step in Tubsey and Hyder and here we are two seasons deep, with a cookbook.

They went from three childhood friends to three TV chefs who aren't the typical culinary faces seen on screen. Instead, they are a fresh palate, a new scope and a driving force behind a change in the food world, inspiring young people to cook and making the older generation laugh along the way.

Unlike traditional food shows, these three embrace their mistakes and provide a representation of authenticity that helps connect people with cooking dishes that may have seemed out of their reach. In a nutshell, if these three can do it, so can you.

Tubsey provides egg cracking and fresh herb chopping to the highest level, but also somehow has the taste buds and vocabulary of a seasoned food critic.

On the other hand, we have Hyder, aka Fryder, a technical cooking master, whose calm, practical and methodical musings tie all the mayhem together in a perfect symphony of flavourisms.

The lads have come together and turned their food knowledge into a 'bad boy piece of information'. From family recipes full of soul that have been passed down through the generations to fast-food mash-ups that are as fun to chef as they are to eat, there's always something delicious and joyful to make.

'This book is for all the mandem and galdem who love food and just need the extra push to stop using Uber Eats at 10pm, and instead start whippin' it in the kitchen. No long.'

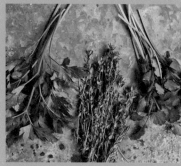

BIG ZUU'S KITCHEN CUPBOARD

All Purpose Seasoning
If you're gunna question the reasoning, wait 'til you taste this seasoning. If there's only one spice mix in your kitchen cupboard, make sure it's this blend of happiness.

Brown sugar
Essential for caramelisation, a nice way to uplift the sourness in tomatoes and just a really good ingredient to have in your house. Also healthier for you in tea.

Buffalo mozzarella
Put on top of any pasta, bake it for extra goodness or dash it in a fresh salad.

Chickpeas
For falafel, curry, hummus. Or just roast, season and thank me later.

Fresh herbs
Coriander, mint, parsley, basil, thyme and rosemary. I never thought I would say this, but these herbs bring life to any dish.

Fufu flour
Everyone has their own version of fufu and it can be made with various types of flour, so buy to suit your taste. If you don't know wag1, buy some cassava flour and follow the instructions on the packet, or keep reading.

Lemon
Great way to season stuff and never underestimate the power of the zest. Hang tight, Richard Blackwood.

Maggi Seasoning cubes
This is the flavour of West Africa in a cube, and every kitchen cupboard will benefit from its presence.

Packet noodles
Whip up a quick ting – simply follow the packet instructions and enjoy, or pimp them up with some leftovers, or keep reading and soon you'll be deep-frying them and turning them into burger buns.

Peanut butter
Great for a sandwich, also quintessential to Sierra Leonean stews.

Roux
Always be ready to roux. You need flour, butter and milk. Use a wooden spoon; it's not a whisk ting.

Scotch bonnets
The chilli flavour lords – sweet, spicy and a real base for Caribbean and African cooking. Basically, if you wanna be black, buy the pepper.

Soy sauce
A secret liquid seasoning, a big boss of Asian cuisine and a nice way to glaze boring boiled broccoli.

Supermalt
The drink I grew up on – a West African staple. This, combined with jollof rice, is a match made in heaven. Always serve stone cold.

 For all you vegans out there, look out for the 'V-Gang' stamp

SNACKS TO SHARE

We ain't talking little bowls of crisps and sweets

JOLLOF RICE BALLS WITH SCOTCH BONNET SAUCE

MAKES: **8**

PREP: **10 MINUTES**

CHILL: **20 MINUTES**

COOK: **15 MINUTES**

400g leftover Mumma Zuu's Jollof Rice (see page 62)

60g mozzarella, cut into 8 pieces and drained well

1.5l vegetable oil, for deep-frying (if using a saucepan; if using a deep-fat fryer follow manufacturer's instructions for oil)

50g plain flour

2 eggs, beaten

50g panko breadcrumbs

1 quantity of Scotch Bonnet Sauce (see page 167)

We have taken the most African dish and gentrified it, but don't worry, my Sierra Leonean elders gave me a pass, and it also tastes nice. This is an embodiment of my love for West African and Italian food. Finally they've come together to create this mighty ball of tastiness.

Divide the leftover Jollof into 8 patties. Take a patty in the palm of your hand and place a piece of mozzarella in the centre. Wrap the rice around it using your hand and shape into a ball. Repeat with the rest of the balls and chill in the fridge for 15–20 minutes.

Preheat the oil in deep-fat fryer to 170°C or heat the oil in a deep saucepan over a medium-high heat to 170°C.

Put the flour, beaten eggs and panko in three shallow dishes. Roll each rice ball in the flour, then egg and then panko, coating well.

Carefully drop the rice balls in the fryer or saucepan and, working in batches, fry for 3–4 minutes until golden brown. Drain well on kitchen paper and serve immediately with Scotch Bonnet Sauce.

ZFC (ZUU FRIED CHICKEN)

SERVES: **4**

PREP: **20 MINUTES**

MARINADE: **2+ HOURS**

COOK: **20 MINUTES**

500g chicken tender or nuggets, or chicken legs or drumsticks or wings

2l vegetable oil, for deep-frying (if using a saucepan; if using a deep-fat fryer follow manufacturer's instructions for oil)

salt and ground black pepper, to taste

FOR THE BRINE FOR CHICKEN TENDERS OR NUGGETS:

100ml buttermilk

1 tsp garlic powder

½ tsp onion powder

½ tsp paprika

1 tsp salt

FOR THE BRINE FOR CHICKEN LEGS OR DRUMSTICKS OR WINGS

250ml buttermilk

1½ tsp garlic powder

1 tsp onion powder

1 tsp paprika

1½ tsp salt

*NOTE: DOUBLE THE DREDGE QUANTITIES IF USING LEGS, DRUMSTICKS OR WINGS

I grew up on fried chicken. I am black, yes, but we can all agree we would take a bullet for the Colonel's secret 11 herbs and spices recipe. Although I may not have my own thriving chicken franchise, these recipes will give you the power to become your own bossman.

DORITOS FRIED CHICKEN

This was on the first episode of *Big Eats* and became a signature dish of the series. The recipe then went viral after a young man's father expressed his admiration for his son's new-found love of cooking, which was ignited by seeing people like me, Tubsey and Hyder cheffing it up on the telly.

FOR THE DREDGE*

50g plain flour

25g cornflour

25g rice flour

50g Doritos, blitzed in a food processor or finely crushed, plus extra Doritos to garnish

MAGGI FRIED CHICKEN (MFC)

Here's some fried chicken that we sent on a tour of West Africa. What they established on their journey was that the Maggi cube is the quintessential essence of West African cuisine. This beautiful little block of all-purpose seasoning will bring to your chicken what it's been missing.

FOR THE DREDGE*

50g plain flour

25g cornflour

25g rice flour

1 Maggi or other vegetable stock cube

½ tsp chilli powder

50g roasted peanuts, finely chopped, to garnish

GOLDEN NUGGETS

Do you know why there are three white bruddas on the front of a Rice Krispies box, but only one chicken on a box of cornflakes? Me neither, but I did fry some chicken nuggets with Rice Krispies and it came out pretty good.

FOR THE DREDGE*

80g rice flour

40g rice cereal (e.g. Rice Krispies), blitzed in a food processor or finely crushed

20g panko breadcrumbs

To make the brine, mix the buttermilk with the garlic powder, onion powder, paprika and salt in a large bowl. Add the chicken and mix well to coat in the brine, then cover and marinate for at least 2 hours and up to 12 hours in the fridge.

For chicken tenders or nuggets, preheat the oil in a deep-fat fryer to 165°C or heat the oil in a deep saucepan over a low-medium heat to 165°C.

For chicken wings or legs and drumsticks, preheat the oil in a deep-fat fryer to 140°C or heat the oil in a deep saucepan over a low heat to 140°C.

To dredge the chicken, mix all your chosen dredge ingredients together in a large bowl. Using tongs, dip the chicken pieces into the dredge, moving them around to coat very well.

To cook tenders or nuggets, carefully move the pieces from the dredge into the hot oil, working in batches. Fry for 4–5 minutes until golden brown and cooked through. Drain on kitchen paper, season and serve.

To cook wings or legs or drumsticks, carefully move the pieces from the dredge into the hot oil, working in batches. Fry for 12–15 minutes, turning a few times during cooking to make sure the coating is browning evenly. When golden brown and cooked through (the interior temperature of chicken should be above 72°C when measured with a meat thermometer, or insert the tip of a knife or skewer into the thickest part; the juices will run clear if it is cooked – if you see any trace of pink, carry on frying or, if they are well browned on the outside, transfer to a foil-lined baking tray and cook for a further 10 minutes in an oven preheated to 195°C/175°C fan/Gas 5), drain on kitchen paper, season and rest for 5 minutes before serving.

Play with your favourite flavours! You can add spices and textures to the brine or dredge for delicious variations.

CRISPY ZUUDLE BALLS

MAKES: **8**

PREP: **15 MINUTES**

CHILL: **30 MINUTES**

COOK: **10 MINUTES**

100g pack instant noodles

2 heaped tbsp gram flour

1 tsp curry powder

1 red chilli, finely chopped

3 spring onions, finely sliced in rounds, plus extra to serve

small handful of coriander, chopped

1l vegetable oil, for deep-frying (if using a saucepan; if using a deep-fat fryer follow manufacturer's instructions for oil)

TO SERVE:

Japanese-style mayonnaise (e.g. Kewpie)

sriracha sauce

Can't say I ever thought I'd deep-fry noodles, but guess what, it happened and Phil Wang loved them. We've all got packet noodles in the cupboard and sometimes we get hungry, boil some water, cook them up and Bob's your uncle, auntie, sister, brother. But hear this, we've created a way for you to take them to a whole new level and created the Crispy Zuudle Balls.

Set the noodle seasoning to one side and cook the instant noodles according to the packet instructions, then drain well, cover and leave to cool in the fridge for 30 minutes.

In a large bowl, mix the noodle seasoning with the gram flour and curry powder, then add the chilli, spring onions, coriander and cold noodles and mix until it becomes a sticky ball. Using wet hands, roll the mixture into 8 small balls and chill in the fridge for 30 minutes.

Preheat the oil in the deep-fat fry to 180°C or heat the oil in a deep saucepan over medium-high heat to 180°C. Fry the noodle balls until golden, drain on kitchen paper and serve drizzled with mayo and sriracha sauce and topped with some extra sliced spring onions.

BITTERBALLEN

1 tbsp vegetable oil

1 shallot, finely chopped

300g beef mince

60g butter

60g plain flour

350ml hot beef stock

fresh nutmeg

handful of parsley, finely chopped

75g plain flour

2 eggs, beaten

100g panko breadcrumbs

1.5l vegetable oil, for deep-frying (if using a saucepan; if using a deep-fat fryer, follow the manufacturer's instructions for oil)

1 tbsp Dijon mustard

2 tbsp mayonnaise

salt and ground black pepper, to taste

ZUU HACKS

When coating the balls, use one hand for dry stages – flour and breadcrumbs – and keep the other hand for the wet egg stage.

When I met Jamali Maddix, he told me about these bitterballen. I didn't know what he was talking about. Little did I know, it was a dish that required a Roux Lord, a bit of minced meat and some serious deep-fryage, creating a truly emotional snack. Don't thank me for this dish, thank Jamali.

Heat the oil in a frying pan over a medium heat and cook the shallot for 5–8 minutes until it is beginning to go golden. Then turn up the heat and add the mince, breaking it up with a wooden spoon. Cook the mince, stirring every so often, until any liquid has evaporated and the meat is starting to caramelise – around 10 minutes.

In a separate saucepan, warm the butter over a medium heat until melted, then add the flour and whisk in to form a roux. Continue cooking and whisking the roux for 2 minutes before gradually adding the hot stock, whisking it in on each addition until it forms a thick sauce.

Add the cooked mince mixture, some grated nutmeg and the parsley. Mix everything together, then season. Tip into a flat dish and cover the surface with clingfilm; the clingfilm touching the mixture will prevent a skin forming. Chill in the fridge for 1½ hours until completely cold and firm.

Remove from the fridge and roll the mixture into 12 walnut-sized balls. In three shallow dishes place the flour, beaten eggs and panko breadcrumbs. Working in batches, roll the balls in the flour, then completely coat in the egg, before rolling in the breadcrumbs and transferring to a baking sheet lined with baking parchment. You can cook these immediately or you can chill in the fridge for up to 3 days, or freeze for up to 1 month at this stage.

When ready to fry, either preheat the oil in a deep-fat fryer to 170°C or heat the oil in a deep saucepan over a medium–high heat to 170°C.

Meanwhile, mix the mustard and mayonnaise together in small bowl.

Fry the bitterballen in batches, turning with tongs as they cook, until they are golden brown. Carefully remove from the oil and drain on kitchen paper for a minute or so before serving with the mustard mayo.

CHEESE 'N' PICKLE POPPERS

MAKES: **12**

PREP: **15 MINUTES**

CHILL: **30 MINUTES**

COOK: **10 MINUTES**

60g soft goats' cheese

80g grated mozzarella

80g extra-mature Cheddar, grated

1 pickle or gherkin, finely chopped and patted dry with kitchen paper

½ tsp mustard powder

1.5l vegetable oil, for deep-frying (if using a saucepan; if using a deep-fat fryer follow manufacturer's instructions for oil)

150g plain flour

2 eggs, beaten

150g panko breadcrumbs

salt and ground black pepper, to taste

TO SERVE:

1 tbsp dried chives

sea salt

Aight boom, I made this one for my bae. She is a cheese and pickle lover, so I united them as sister and brother, in a hot bath of oil. Through creating these oozing balls of cheese and happiness, I've found a better use for pickles than just tossing them straight in the bin.

In a bowl, mix the cheeses, diced pickle or gherkin and mustard powder together with a little salt and pepper. Roll the mix into 12 small balls and chill on a baking sheet lined with baking parchment in the fridge for 30 minutes.

Preheat the oil in a deep-fat fryer to 180°C or heat the oil in a deep saucepan over a medium-high heat to 180°C.

Place the flour, beaten eggs and breadcrumbs in three separate shallow dishes. Working in batches, coat each ball in the flour, then egg, then breadcrumbs. Then return the balls to the egg and coat again, followed by the breadcrumbs for a super-crunchy coating.

When the oil is hot, fry the poppers in batches for 2 minutes until golden brown. Drain on kitchen paper. Serve dusted in the dried chives and with a sprinkle of sea salt.

Double-dip your poppers in the eggs and breadcrumbs for an extra-crispy bite.

SALT 'N' PEPPER SQUID

SERVES: **4**

PREP: **20 MINUTES**

COOK: **10 MINUTES**

400g squid, cleaned and sliced into rings

¼ tsp white pepper

1 tsp Chinese five spice

80g cornflour

½ tsp fine salt

2l vegetable oil, for deep-frying (if using a saucepan; if using a deep-fat fryer follow manufacturer's instructions for oil), plus 1 tbsp vegetable oil, for frying

1 red chilli, sliced

1 green chilli, sliced

2 garlic cloves, sliced

2 spring onions, sliced

½ tsp Szechuan peppercorns, crushed

Where do I begin... if I could order something forever from every restaurant, it would be this. I don't know what it is about the salt and peppery goodness of salt 'n' pepper squid, but I come back every time and, even though I now cook it, I will still get it delivered to my yard.

Dry off the squid pieces as much as possible with some kitchen paper, then mix the white pepper and Chinese five spice together in a bowl and marinade the squid in it for a few minutes.

Mix together the cornflour and salt. Preheat the oil in a deep-fat fryer to 190°C or heat the oil in a deep saucepan over a high heat to 190°C.

When the oil is hot, toss the squid in the cornflour and salt mixture until really well coated. Then fry the squid in the searingly hot oil - be careful as it may spit! Do this in batches so as not to overcrowd the pan and reduce the oil temperature. Fry the squid for 1-2 minutes until golden brown, then drain on kitchen paper.

While the squid is cooking, heat the 1 tablespoon of vegetable oil in a wok or large frying pan over a medium heat and fry the chillies, garlic, spring onions and Szechuan pepper together until fragrant - about 1 minute. Toss this mixture with the crispy fried squid and serve immediately.

JAMAICAN BEEF PATTIES

MAKES: **6**

PREP: **15 MINUTES**

CHILL: **1 HOUR**

COOK: **40 MINUTES**

½ onion, quartered

3 spring onions, chopped

1 garlic clove

1.5cm piece fresh root ginger, peeled

1 tbsp thyme

1 Scotch bonnet chilli

½ tsp salt

½ tsp ground black pepper

1 tsp paprika

½ tsp allspice

1 tsp hot Caribbean curry powder

1 tsp onion powder

1 tsp garlic powder

4 tbsp vegetable oil

200g beef mince

1 tbsp gravy browning

200ml beef stock

20g fresh breadcrumbs

FOR THE PASTRY:

250g plain flour, plus extra for dusting

½ tsp baking powder

1 tsp sugar

½ tsp salt

1 tsp turmeric

1 tsp hot Caribbean curry powder

125g vegetable shortening, very cold, diced

60g vegetable suet

2 eggs, beaten

This is a hard one to get right, but luckily YouTube is amazing – the authentic chef, Andre Fowles, shared this recipe on VICE and I've used it as inspiration for this dish. Now you can all enjoy the patty experience I used to get at my local Caribbean shop growing up in West London.

Start by making the beef mixture. In a food processor, blend the onion, spring onions, garlic, ginger, thyme, Scotch bonnet, salt, pepper, spices, curry powder, onion and garlic powders and 2 tablespoons of the oil to make a paste.

Heat the remaining oil in a large frying pan and add the paste, frying over a medium heat for 15 minutes until dark and fragrant. Add the mince and break up really well in the pan using a wooden spoon, frying until all the meat has evenly browned. Then add the gravy browning and beef stock and bring up to a simmer. Take off the heat and mix in the breadcrumbs, check the seasoning and leave to cool, then place in the fridge for 1 hour or until completely cold.

For the pastry, add the flour, baking powder, sugar, salt, turmeric and curry powder to a food processor or large bowl.

If you are using a food processor, pulse to combine, then add the shortening and suet and pulse until the mixture resembles breadcrumbs. Add half the beaten eggs and 2 tablespoons water and pulse to form a crumbly dough. Bring together with your hands, then wrap in clingfilm and put in the fridge to rest for 30 minutes.

If you are making the pastry by hand, add the shortening and suet to the dry ingredients and rub in with your fingers until the mixture resembles breadcrumbs. Add half the beaten egg and 2 tablespoons water and use a butter knife to combine the wet and dry ingredients before bringing the dough together with your hands. Wrap in clingfilm and put in the fridge to rest.

Preheat the oven to 220°C/200°C fan/Gas 7 and line two baking sheets with baking parchment. Remove the pastry from the fridge and roll out to a thickness of about 0.5cm. Cut out 6 x 6cm rounds using a cutter or bowl.

Place 3 tablespoons of the cooled beef mixture in the middle of each round and brush the edges of the rounds with the remaining beaten egg. Fold half the pastry over the meat and press to seal the edges with a fork. Transfer to the baking sheets and bake for 15 minutes until the edges of the pastry are just turning golden.

ZUU HACKS

Deep-fry leftover pieces of dough for a crazy crunchy snack.

BÖREK ALGÉRIENNE

MAKES: **12**

PREP: **20 MINUTES**

COOK: **50 MINUTES**

1 tbsp olive oil

1 onion, diced

1 tsp chilli flakes

½ tsp ground cinnamon

½ tsp ground cumin

400g beef mince

4 tbsp cream cheese

handful of parsley, finely chopped

20g butter

4 eggs, beaten

1.5l vegetable oil, for deep-frying (if using a saucepan; if using a deep-fat fryer follow manufacturer's instructions for oil)

6 sheets filo pastry or 12 spring roll wrappers

salt and ground black pepper, to taste

TO SERVE:

lemon wedges, for squeezing over

chilli sauce

I love North African food and somehow they make better spring rolls than any Chinese version I've ever had. A Ramadan speciality, this one always makes me look forward to breaking fast. Best enjoyed with a squeeze of lemon.

Heat the olive oil in a large frying pan and cook the onion over a medium heat for 10–15 minutes. Then add the spices and the beef mince and fry, using a wooden spoon to break the mince up. Cook until any liquid has completely evaporated and the mince is brown. Remove from the heat and leave to cool completely. When cool, mix in 2 tablespoons of the cream cheese and the parsley and season well.

In a non-stick omelette or frying pan, heat the butter until just foaming. Season the beaten eggs with a pinch of salt and pepper and pour into the pan (put the bowl to one side as you will need the dregs of the beaten egg to seal the filo pastry later). Use a fork to whisk the egg slightly before letting it settle and set as an omelette. Remove from the pan and leave to cool. When the omelette is cool, cut into 12 pieces.

Preheat the oil in a deep-fat fryer to 180°C or heat the oil in a deep saucepan over a medium-high heat to 180°C.

Meanwhile, lay out one sheet of filo in front of you horizontally, keeping the other sheets covered in a clean, damp tea towel.

Cut the filo in two widthways, so you now have two strips with their shortest edge nearest to you. Spread a small amount of the remaining cream cheese on the filo. Then place 1 heaped tablespoon of the beef mixture at the end nearest to you. Top the beef with a piece of the omelette. Fold over the sides, then roll the beef mixture end away from you to form a sort of cigar shape. Brush the end with some of the remaining beaten egg to seal, then set aside. Repeat with the other piece of filo from that sheet and then repeat with the remaining filo sheets.

When you are ready to fry, working in batches, gently place the böreks in the oil and turn a few times. Fry for 4–5 minutes until golden and crisp, then drain on kitchen paper. Serve immediately with lemon wedges and your favourite chilli sauce!

LEBANESE SAUSAGE ROLLS

MAKES: **8 REGULAR OR 16 MINI**

PREP: **30 MINUTES**

CHILL: **1 HOUR 10 MINUTES**

COOK: **35 MINUTES**

1 tbsp olive oil

1 onion, finely chopped

2 garlic cloves, grated

1 tbsp tomato paste

3 tbsp ras el hanout

500g lamb mince

1 tbsp dried mint

small bunch of coriander, finely chopped

30g soft white breadcrumbs

½ tsp fine salt

2 sheets ready-rolled puff pastry

1 egg, beaten

2 tbsp white sesame seeds

2 tbsp black sesame seeds

ground black pepper

TO SERVE:

chilli sauce

pickles

Greggs sorted out the vegans, but they didn't cover the Akhis. Don't worry, we here at *Big Zuu's Big Eats* have created a meaty sausage roll that my brothers and sisters can enjoy, while adding a Lebanese twist for extra pleasure.

Heat the oil in a frying pan, add the onion and fry over a medium heat for 8 minutes until browned and softened. Add the grated garlic, tomato paste and ras el hanout and cook for 2 more minutes before removing from the pan and cooling in the fridge for 10 minutes.

Once cooled, add it to a large bowl along with the mince, mint, coriander, breadcrumbs, salt, some pepper and 20ml water.

Take half the mixture and form it into a sausage shape along the long side of one of the sheets of puff pastry, leaving a 2cm border. Brush the border with some of the beaten egg and then roll over the pastry to seal tightly on the other side. Trim the excess pastry, then cut into 4 pieces for large koftas or 8 pieces for mini ones. Repeat with the remaining meat and other sheet of pastry.

Arrange the rolls on a baking sheet lined with baking parchment. Using a chopstick or fork, crimp the edges on each roll to tightly seal. Brush each roll all over with the remaining beaten egg and sprinkle with a mix of the sesame seeds. Chill in the fridge for 1 hour.

Preheat the oven to 200°C/180°C fan/Gas 6. Bake the sausage rolls for 25 minutes until cooked through. Leave to cool slightly before serving. Serve with your favourite chilli sauce and some pickles.

STARTERS

So good your main ting will be worried

THE JHEEZE STRAW

SERVES: **4**

PREP: **20 MINUTES**

COOK: **35 MINUTES**

250g Camembert,
in the box

1 sheet ready-rolled puff
pastry

1 tbsp honey, plus extra
for drizzling

2 tsp thyme leaves

1 tbsp grated Parmesan

1 egg, beaten

salt and ground black
pepper, to taste

Bare cheese, bare greeze, this will leave the crowd pleased. The mandem don't really know about cheese like that, apart from Cheddar, Parmesan and maybe mozzarella, if we are moving boujie. So, when we unlocked the Camembert and its baked goodness potential, we needed to find the perfect dipping partner. STEP IN puff pastry that we bought from a shop, elevated that quickly and now we present the whitest dish we have ever made.

Preheat the oven to 200°C/180°C fan/Gas 6.

Take the Camembert out of the box and remove any wrapping. Discard the lid and put the empty base of the box in the middle of a baking sheet lined with baking parchment.

Unroll the puff pastry sheet and drizzle with the honey, then sprinkle over 1 teaspoon of the thyme leaves, the Parmesan and some salt and pepper.

Roll the longest side of the sheet away from you to form a long log. Gently stretch the pastry log longer by lifting it up and lightly tapping down on the worktop so that it measures roughly 50cm. Then cut the log in two lengthways, leaving about 2.5cm at one end intact, so it forms two thinner strands, still joined at that end. Twist the pieces of pastry together to form a plait, then wrap around the Camembert box and seal the ends together well to form a wreath. Brush with the beaten egg and to bake for 15 minutes.

Take the baking sheet out of the oven and place the Camembert back into the box. Return to the oven for another 20 minutes until the pastry is puffed and golden and the Camembert molten and oozing. Serve immediately drizzled with some more honey and sprinkled with the remaining thyme.

OLD SKL CHEESE 'N' TOMATO PASTRIES

MAKES: **6**

PREP: **25 MINUTES**

COOK: **30 MINUTES**

2 plum tomatoes, each sliced into 6

100g passata

1 tsp tomato paste

1½ tsp dried oregano

1½ tsp dried rosemary

150g grated mozzarella

50g Cheddar, grated

350g roll ready-made chilled croissant dough

1 tbsp grated Parmesan

salt and ground black pepper, to taste

Imagine man's in school, it's break-time, I got 80p. Do I sacrifice the money for a beautiful hot snack before lunch? Or do I keep my bread and use it to buy a KA and sweets after school? This was my constant struggle growing up. Not gonna lie, the pastry often won. Such a simple dish but, when made correctly, leads to so much joy you will have these in your house for standard.

Preheat the oven to 200°C/180°C fan/Gas 6.

Lay the tomato slices on kitchen paper to dry out slightly. Mix together the passata, tomato paste, 1 teaspoon each of the oregano and rosemary and some salt and pepper. Mix together the mozzarella and Cheddar.

Unroll the croissant dough and separate each croissant piece along the perforated edge. Spread 1 tablespoon of the passata mixture in the centre of a triangle, then top with a slice of tomato. Fold over the middle point of the triangle. Then add a handful of the mixed cheeses and fold over the other two points to form a little rectangular parcel. Press the points together gently to seal and place on a baking sheet lined with baking parchment.

Repeat for the remaining triangles, then bake for 20 minutes. Remove from the oven and top each pastry with another slice of tomato and sprinkle over the remaining herbs and the Parmesan. Return to the oven for 10 minutes. Serve hot from the oven!

SAUSAGE & EGG MUSLAMIC MUFFINS

MAKES: **4**

PREP: **15 MINUTES**

COOK: **15 MINUTES**

250g turkey mince

30g soft white breadcrumbs

½ tsp All Purpose Seasoning

½ tsp dried rosemary, finely crushed

½ tsp dried thyme, finely crushed

¼ tsp fine salt

1 tbsp whole milk

4 English muffins, sliced in half

20g butter, for spreading

4 tbsp vegetable oil

4 eggs

4 slices of burger cheese

salt and ground black pepper, to taste

When I first realised that the McDonald's sausage was made from pork, it broke my heart. I couldn't imagine living in a world where I could never eat it again. LUCKILY, my Akhis came together to create a version the world could experience without going to Dubai or Morocco.

Combine the mince, breadcrumbs, All Purpose Seasoning, dried herbs, salt and milk in a bowl, but don't overmix! Split the mixture into 4 patties and shape into 10cm rounds.

Toast and butter the muffins. Preheat the grill to medium.

Fry the patties in 2 tablespoons of the vegetable oil in a large frying pan over a medium heat until golden brown and firm on both sides.

Grease 4 x 8cm cooking rings and place in a non-stick frying pan with the remaining vegetable oil over a low-medium heat. Crack an egg into each ring and gently fry for 3 minutes. The bottom half of the egg will set but the top half will still be soft. Then cover the pan with a lid or tray and leave to steam for another 3-4 minutes. This will just cook the white of the egg but leave the yolk runny.

Meanwhile, place a slice of burger cheese on the bottom half of each muffin and place under the grill to gently melt.

When the eggs are cooked, gently release them from their moulds. Plate your muffin: top the bottom cheesy muffin half with a turkey patty and then an egg, then season with salt and pepper before sandwiching with the top slice of muffin. Serve immediately.

Make your turkey patty slightly wider than the muffin – it will shrink in cooking and then fit perfectly.

THE FRENCH TACO

SERVES: **2**

PREP: **20 MINUTES**

COOK: **25 MINUTES**

6 chicken breast mini fillets, about 250g

2 tbsp olive oil

½ tsp garlic powder

½ tsp smoked paprika

½ tsp ground cumin

½ tsp dried oregano

2 merguez sausages

½ red pepper, thinly sliced

½ green pepper, thinly sliced

2 large tortillas

Sauce Algérienne
(see page 172)

100g grated mozzarella

2 tbsp Nacho Cheese Sauciness (see page 170)

2 handfuls of cooked oven chips

2 spring onions, sliced

50g pickled jalapeños

salt and ground black pepper, to taste

The French took a Mexican dish, named it incorrectly and basically swapped the rice and beans in a burrito with chips and cheese. Bare meat combined with hella flavours in a massive tortilla, then pressed in a grill – it's very mad. When I went to Paris and had this, it made me question the fast-food levels in the UK.

Place the chicken fillets in a large bowl together with 1 tablespoon of the oil, the garlic powder, smoked paprika, ground cumin, oregano and some salt and pepper.

Heat the remaining oil in a frying pan over a medium heat. Slice the merguez in half lengthways and fry for 3-4 minutes, turning after the cut sides are golden and crisp. Once cooked, set aside and add the chicken fillets and sliced peppers to the pan. Fry over a medium heat for 8-10 minutes until the chicken fillets are golden brown on all sides and firm, and the peppers are soft and lightly charred.

Spread a layer of Sauce Algérienne in the centre of one tortilla, then sprinkle over a quarter of the mozzarella. Top with half the merguez, followed by 3 chicken fillets and half the peppers. Add a spoonful of Nacho Cheese Sauciness, half the chips, half the spring onions and half the jalapeños. Top with another quarter of the mozzarella and season with salt and pepper. Fold in the edges of the tortilla over the filling to create a rectangle. Repeat to make the other wrap.

If you have a panini press, heat on medium. When it's hot, add the wraps, folded-side down, and cook for 5-8 minutes until the outside is golden and crisp and the cheese is melted.

If you are using a griddle, heat it over a low heat. Place the wraps folded-side down on the griddle and weight them down with a heavy dish. Cook for 4-5 minutes on each side.

RAMEN NOODLE SLIDERS

SERVES: **4**

PREP: **25 MINUTES**

CHILL: **30+ MINUTES**

COOK: **20 MINUTES**

200g instant noodles

1 egg, beaten

2 tbsp vegetable oil

200g beef mince

1 tbsp miso paste

1 tsp soy sauce

1 tsp sesame oil

2 Cheddar cheese slices, quartered

sriracha, Japanese-style mayonnaise (e.g. Kewpie), mustard or any of your favourite condiments

1 Little Gem lettuce, finely sliced

2 spring onions, finely shredded

100g kimchi

Using the lid to steam the cheese on the burgers results in a perfectly cooked, juicy cheeseburger.

Billin' up a burger with noodles as the bun is the kind of mad food you will see scrolling through your Instagram feed. Giving you the cheffy powers to make this in your own kitchen and proving no idea is too crazy is what we love. But at this point you are reading a cookbook written by a Grime MC, so anything is possible.

Cook the instant noodles with their seasoning according to the packet instructions, then drain well, cover and place in the fridge to cool. Once cooled, mix together with the beaten egg.

Grease 8 holes of a shallow muffin tin with 1 tablespoon of the vegetable oil. Fill each hole with a handful of the noodle mixture, pressing down firmly so that it is flat and tightly packed. Chill in the fridge for a minimum of 30 minutes.

Preheat the oven to 200°C/180°C fan/Gas 6.

For the burgers, mix together the mince with the miso paste, soy sauce and sesame oil and shape into 4 patties. Flatten the patties well until they are slightly wider than the holes in the muffin tray as they will shrink when cooking.

Remove the noodle 'buns' from the fridge and bake in the oven for 12–15 minutes until lightly golden and firm.

Meanwhile, in a frying pan that has a lid, heat the remaining oil over a medium heat, then add the burger patties. Press the patties down with a spatula as they cook to get a delicious crust. Cook for 3 minutes on one side, then flip and top each patty with half a cheese slice. Cover the pan with the lid and cook for another 2–3 minutes until the cheese is melted. Place the burgers on a plate to rest.

Remove the noodle buns from the oven and carefully remove from the muffin tin.

To make each slider, drizzle the condiment of your choice on a base noodle bun, then top with lettuce and spring onions. Then add a cheeseburger, followed by a spoonful of spicy kimchi. Place the second bun on top and secure with a cocktail stick. Serve with a cold beer.

KOREAN FRIED CHICKEN (KFC)

SERVES: **4**

PREP: **20 MINUTES**

MARINADE: **2+ HOURS**

COOK: **20 MINUTES**

4 garlic cloves, grated

2.5cm piece fresh root ginger, peeled and grated

3 tbsp rice wine vinegar

1 tsp fine salt

1kg chicken wings, split into drumettes and wingettes

1.5l vegetable oil, for deep-frying (if using a saucepan; if using a deep-fat fryer follow manufacturer's instructions for oil)

100g cornflour

FOR THE KOREAN GLAZE:

60g gochujang paste or sriracha if you can't find gochujang

60g ketchup

40g clear honey

1 tbsp brown sugar

1 tbsp soy sauce

1 tbsp rice wine vinegar

1 tsp sesame oil

TO SERVE:

4 spring onions, sliced

2 tbsp toasted sesame seeds

I never knew KFC in Korea meant a whole other thing. But now I've found out that they took fried chicken and coated it in a sauce, and it's elevated my entire mouth experience.

In a large bowl, mix the garlic and ginger with the rice wine vinegar and salt. Add the wings and mix really well to coat, then chill for 2 hours minimum to marinate.

When you are ready to cook, preheat the oil in your deep-fat fryer to 160°C or heat the oil in a deep saucepan over a medium heat to 160°C.

While the oil is heating make the glaze. Mix together all the ingredients in a saucepan and bring to the boil. Simmer for 5 minutes until thick and glossy. Keep warm.

Place the cornflour in a large shallow bowl. When the oil is hot, toss the marinated wings in the cornflour. Do this in batches to make it easier to coat well.

Fry the wings in batches for 10-12 minutes until golden brown and cooked through. Insert the tip of a knife or a skewer into the thickest part of one: the juices will run clear if it is cooked. Place the hot glaze in a large bowl.

Remove the wings from the oil using tongs and immediately toss in the spicy Korean glaze. Serve immediately dressed with the spring onions and toasted sesame seeds.

If you don't want to fry the wings, toss in 2 tablespoons vegetable oil and roast at 245°C/225°C fan/Gas 9 for 25 minutes. Then coat in the hot glaze and serve.

G.O.A.T. NACHOS

SERVES: **6**

PREP: **30 MINUTES**

COOK: **5 HOURS 10 MINUTES**

1.4kg bone-in goat or lamb shoulder

200g salted tortilla chips

150g grated mozzarella

150g Red Leicester, grated

salt

FOR THE PASTE:

2 tbsp chipotle paste

1 tbsp ground cumin

1 tbsp smoked paprika

25g honey

1–2 fresh red chillies, depending on how hot you like it

2 tsp salt

4 garlic cloves, crushed

1 onion, chopped

400g tin plum tomatoes

400ml lamb or chicken stock

This is one of the pengest things we made on *Big Eats*. Slow pulled goat (or lamb) over nachos, with all the extra happiness, equals an emotional food exchange. It's not limited to nachos, but I think the way the crunchy tortilla chips take on the jelly-like meat gold creates a vibe that can only be done with this recipe.

Preheat the oven to 150˚C/130˚C fan/Gas 2.

Make the paste. Blend all the ingredients together in a food processor, then rub all over the meat.

Place in a roasting tin, cover with foil and slow-roast for 4 hours. Remove foil and continue to cook for a further 1 hour until the meat is super-tender and comes off the bone easily. Shred the meat from the bone using two forks and mix with the spicy pan juices. Keep warm.

Make the guacamole and the salsa by mixing all the ingredients together and seasoning well with salt.

Preheat the oven to 200˚C/180˚C fan/Gas 6 or heat the grill to high.

Scatter half the tortilla chips over a roasting tray, then top with half the meat and half of the two cheeses. Repeat with the remaining tortilla chips, meat and cheese. Place in the oven or under the grill for 5–8 minutes until the cheese is melted and bubbling and just starting to brown.

To serve, dress with piles of guacamole, salsa, the jalapeños and soured cream, if you like.

FOR THE GUACAMOLE:

1 avocado, smashed

juice of ½ lime

¼ onion, finely chopped

1 red chilli, finely chopped

FOR THE FRESH TOMATO SALSA:

1 large tomato, diced

juice of ½ lime

¼ onion, finely chopped

handful of coriander, roughly chopped

salt

TO SERVE:

2 tbsp pickled jalapeños

100g soured cream (optional)

BANGIN' BBQ WINGS

SERVES: **4**

PREP: **10 MINUTES**

BRINE: **4+ HOURS**

COOK: **25 MINUTES**

1.2kg chicken wings

1 tsp vegetable oil

½ quantity of Bangin' BBQ Sauce (see page 172), plus extra to serve

FOR THE BRINE:

2l water

60g fine salt

30g caster sugar

2 bay leaves

2 sprigs of thyme

1 tsp coriander seeds, crushed

2 cloves

1 Scotch bonnet chilli, halved (optional)

½ tsp white pepper

Use this brine for any chicken on the bone. It adds amazing flavour to the meat and keeps it moist when cooking.

I love wings, it was a cut me and my friends could afford when we were 16. Hungry and wanting something different to eat, I would keep it simple with basic seasoning, then bang them in the oven. But over time I learnt how to really make the most out of the humble wing, so it was just as good as fillet steak. Good BBQ wings ain't easy to come by, but if you follow this recipe you have my word that they will be better than the BBQ wings from Pizza Hut.

Add all the brine ingredients to a large saucepan over a high heat and bring to the boil. As soon as the liquid boils take off the heat and leave to cool completely. Once cool, pour into a large bowl or plastic container, add the wings, cover and chill in the fridge for 4–6 hours.

Preheat a griddle pan over a medium heat, or preheat the oven to 240°C/220°C fan/Gas 9. You can also barbecue these wings.

Remove the wings from the brine and pat dry. Discard the brine.

If you are griddling or barbecuing, place the wings on the griddle or on the barbecue and leave untouched for 8 minutes before turning. Repeat on the other side, then brush lightly with some of the BBQ Sauce and continue to cook, turning frequently to avoid burning the glaze. Continue until the wings have a light char and dark glaze and the meat is cooked through – about 25 minutes total.

If you are using the oven, place the wings on a tray lined with foil and drizzle over the oil. Roast for 10 minutes before turning. After 10 minutes on the other side remove from the oven and brush over the BBQ Sauce. Turn the oven to grill on high and grill the wings for 2–3 minutes on each side until they are burnished and brown.

Serve immediately with more Bangin' BBQ Sauce and your favourite sides.

HYDER'S KURDISH SHIFTA

SERVES: **4**

PREP: **20 MINUTES**

COOK: **20 MINUTES**

500g lamb mince

1 plum tomato, grated

1 onion, grated

2 tbsp plain flour

large handful of parsley, finely chopped

1 tbsp ground cumin

1 tsp paprika

½ tsp cayenne pepper

1 tsp salt

100ml vegetable oil, for frying

ground black pepper, to taste

TO SERVE:

salad

flatbreads

yoghurt

Hyder and his dad have never failed to amaze me with their westernised dishes that are actually Iraqi. Here we have a burger that went to Slemani, had some cardamom tea and found some lit spices in a bazaar... and there you have it, the shifta.

In a large bowl, combine the lamb with the tomato, onion, flour, parsley, spices, salt and some pepper.

Take a golfball-size amount of the mixture in the palm of your hand and flatten to form an oval patty. Repeat with the rest of the mixture to make 10-12 patties.

Heat the oil in a large frying pan over a medium heat. Gently lay the patties in the oil and fry for 6-8 minutes on each side until deeply golden. Serve immediately with salad, flatbreads and yoghurt.

STUFFED CABBAGE HIGH ROLLERS

V-GANG

SERVES: **4**

PREP: **20 MINUTES**

COOK: **1 HOUR 10 MINUTES**

FOR THE TOMATO SAUCE:

1 tbsp vegetable oil

1 red onion, finely chopped

1 tbsp ginger paste

1 tbsp garlic paste

1 red chilli, finely chopped

1 tbsp ground cumin

1 tsp turmeric

2 x 400g tins chopped tomatoes

2 bay leaves

1 cinnamon stick

200ml vegetable stock

salt and ground black pepper, to taste

coconut yoghurt, to serve

FOR THE CABBAGE:

250g cooked basmati rice

1 tbsp vegetable oil

½ tsp turmeric

50g raisins

50g desiccated coconut

handful of chopped coriander leaves, plus extra to serve

8 large Savoy cabbage leaves, from 1 large cabbage

A cheeky version of dolma that takes a basic vegetable and turns it into a lil' parcel of greatness. These kind of techie dishes prove man's chef level and will also show people that you can do *Masterchef*-level cookery in your yard, without Gregg and John criticising your plating.

For the sauce, add the oil to a wide saucepan over a medium heat. Fry the red onion for 8-10 minutes until it is golden and soft, then add the ginger and garlic pastes, chilli, cumin and turmeric. Cook for 4-5 minutes, adding a splash of water if the mixture dries out. Then add the tomatoes, bay leaves, cinnamon and vegetable stock and a generous pinch of salt. Leave to simmer gently for 30 minutes while you prepare the cabbage leaves.

Bring a large pan of water to the boil. Separate the cabbage leaves – try to find ones that are all a similar size. Use a knife to remove the thickest part of the white stalk but keep the leaf whole. Boil the leaves in the water for 2 minutes, then drain and cool in iced water.

Mix together the rice, oil, turmeric, raisins, coconut and coriander and season well with salt and pepper. Drain the cabbage leaves well and lay out flat on some kitchen paper. Put 2 heaped tablespoons of the rice mixture in the centre of each leaf. Fold over the edges like a wrap and roll together. Repeat for the rest of the leaves. Carefully place each rolled cabbage leaf into the simmering sauce, seam-side down, and cover with a lid or some foil and poach gently over a low heat for 20 minutes.

Serve the stuffed leaves in the warm sauce with some extra coriander and coconut yoghurt.

BUFFALO BITES WITH RANCH DRESSING

SERVES: **2**

PREP: **15 MINUTES**

COOK: **10 MINUTES**

30g cornflour

15g plain flour

1 tsp garlic powder

½ tsp cayenne pepper

ground black pepper

100ml oat milk

50ml buffalo hot sauce (I use Frank's)

200g seitan pieces

vegetable oil, for frying

1 celery stick, cut into chunks, to serve

FOR THE RANCH DRESSING:

100g vegan mayonnaise

2 tbsp liquid from a jar of pickles

1 tsp dried dill

½ tsp garlic powder

Can't lie, I thought seitan was the devil's work and the first time I saw this ingredient, I still thought it. But sometimes, when cooking for other people, you have to move outside your comfort zone and thanks to Lou Sanders' love of meat substitutes, we ended up with some vegan clouds of pengness.

Mix all the dressing ingredients in a small bowl and set aside.

In a shallow bowl, mix the cornflour, flour, garlic powder, cayenne pepper and a good grind of black pepper. Pour the oat milk into a shallow bowl. Put the buffalo hot sauce in another shallow bowl.

Dip the pieces of seitan in the oat milk, then toss in the seasoned flour to coat.

Add vegetable oil to a frying pan up to 1cm in depth and put over a medium-high heat. Test to see if the oil is hot enough by sprinkling some flour in it – if it sizzles it is ready to go!

Dust off any excess flour and fry the seitan pieces on both sides until golden and crisp. Drain on kitchen paper, then toss in the hot sauce before serving with the ranch dressing and celery chunks.

CHEESEBURGER QUESADILLA

SERVES: **2 AS A STARTER OR 4–6 AS A SNACK**

PREP: **10 MINUTES**

COOK: **15 MINUTES**

2 tsp vegetable oil

200g lean beef mince

2 x 20cm tortilla wraps

4 Red Leicester slices, broken into pieces

¼ onion, finely chopped

1 gherkin, chopped

1 tbsp shredded Little Gem lettuce

1 tbsp American mustard

1 tbsp tomato ketchup

salt and ground black pepper, to taste

Take a dish that's already peng and combine it with another peng dish, what you gonna get? Well, if you slate the contents of a cheeseburger into two tortillas, it's gonna taste dank. I cooked this live on *Sunday Brunch*, which confirmed my TV chef level, so if I can do this with Simon and Tim watching me like hawks, it's going to be totally chilled doing it in your house.

Add 1 teaspoon of the oil to a frying pan and place over a high heat. Fry the mince for 5-8 minutes, seasoning well with salt and pepper. When any excess liquid has evaporated and the mince is starting to crisp, remove from the pan and set aside.

Lay one of the tortilla wraps on the worktop and layer half the cheese pieces evenly over. Spoon the cooked mince on top, then add the onion, gherkin and lettuce. Drizzle the mustard and ketchup over and top with the remaining cheese in an even layer.

Add the remaining teaspoon of oil to a large non-stick frying pan over a low heat. Carefully place the loaded wrap in the pan, then cover with the other wrap and press down firmly. Fry gently for 3-4 minutes until the cheese is melting, then carefully flip the quesadilla and repeat on the other side.

Remove from the heat, cut into 2-6 portions and serve immediately.

SPINACH FATAYER

MAKES: **30**

PREP: **30 MINUTES**

PROVE: **2 HOURS
10 MINUTES**

COOK: **12 MINUTES**

FOR THE DOUGH:

300g strong white bread flour, plus extra for dusting

1 tsp fine salt

140ml warm water

30ml milk

2 tbsp olive oil, plus extra for brushing

7g sachet instant yeast

FOR THE FILLING:

250g spinach, roughly chopped

1 tsp fine salt

1 onion, finely chopped

100g toasted pine nuts

1 tbsp sumac

1 tbsp olive oil

1 tsp pomegranate molasses

This dish is Lebanese tradition made into a triangle. My grandma made these for me when I was in Sierra Leone and I will never forget how nice it was eating a classic Lebanese dish cooked by my Lebanese grandma. In Lebanon these come in all different sizes and flavourings with varying degrees of sourness and saltiness, so have a little go and adjust to suit your taste.

To make the dough, mix the flour and salt together in a large bowl or stand mixer.

Combine the water, milk, oil and yeast together in a jug and mix well. Leave to stand for 5 minutes until cloudy and fizzy.

Make a well in the flour and pour in the wet ingredients. If you are using a mixer, mix the dough slowly with a dough hook to start and then on a medium speed for 5 minutes until smooth and elastic. If you are making the dough by hand, stir to mix the wet and dry ingredients, then use your hands to bring the dough together.

Transfer the dough to a clean surface and knead well for about 5-8 minutes until smooth and elastic. Place in a clean, oiled bowl, cover with clingfilm and leave to prove in a warm place for 2 hours.

To prepare the filling, stir the salt into the spinach and leave to sit for 30 minutes, then place the spinach in a sieve and squeeze out all the liquid. Transfer to a clean bowl, add the remaining ingredients and mix well.

When the dough has proved, preheat the oven to 240°C/220°C fan/Gas 9.

Divide the dough into 30 equal pieces, then roll each into a ball. Dust the worktop with flour and roll each ball of dough into an 8cm thick disc. Put 1 tablespoon of filling in the centre of each disc, then gather the edges of the dough into the centre and pinch together at three points. Press together to seal, then raise the seams with your fingertips.

Transfer to a baking sheet lined with baking paper, brush with oil and bake for 12 minutes until golden.

MEAT & FISH

Mains in different lanes

MUMMA ZUU'S JOLLOF RICE

SERVES: **4–6**

PREP: **20 MINUTES**

COOK: **1 HOUR 40 MINUTES**

800g lamb leg, diced

3 tbsp All Purpose Seasoning

1l vegetable oil, for deep-frying (if using a saucepan; if using a deep-fat fryer, follow manufacturer's instructions for oil), plus 3 tbsp vegetable oil, for frying

1 onion, diced

4 garlic cloves, crushed

1–2 Scotch bonnet chillies, depending on how hot you like it, chopped or whole

4 tbsp tomato paste

600g plum tomatoes, chopped

4 Maggi or other vegetable stock cubes, crushed

2 bay leaves

pinch each of white pepper and ground black pepper

500g basmati rice, rinsed

salt

You guys are lucky, I'm not gonna lie, 'cause this is a sacred recipe and, once you make this, you will make it forever. Everyone has their own version and even right now I guarantee there'll be West Africans debating about who makes the best one. Well, I am here representing Sierra Leone and I'm saying with my chest that we have the best jollof rice in the world. Take me in, try the recipe, then chat to me.

Toss the lamb in 2 tablespoons of the All Purpose Seasoning. Place in a saucepan, cover with cold water and bring up to the boil. Simmer for 40 minutes–1 hour until just tender, skimming off any foam that comes to the surface. Drain the lamb, reserving the cooking liquid. Dry the lamb pieces on kitchen paper.

Preheat the oil in a deep-fat fryer to 170°C or heat the oil in a deep saucepan over a medium-high heat to 170°C. Then, working in batches, carefully fry the pieces of lamb for 2–3 minutes until they are golden brown and crisp all over. Drain on kitchen paper and set aside.

Heat the 3 tablespoons of vegetable oil in a large casserole and add the onion. Cook for 10–15 minutes over a medium heat until the onion is golden, then add the garlic, Scotch bonnets, tomato paste and remaining All Purpose Seasoning. Cook for another 2 minutes before adding the tomatoes, stock cubes, bay leaves, salt and a pinch each of black and white pepper. Simmer for 5 minutes before stirring in the rice and the cooked lamb.

Measure the leftover cooking stock from the lamb into a jug. You need 850ml – if there isn't enough, top up with water. Stir this into the rice, cover with foil, put the lid on and turn the heat down to low. Simmer for 25–30 minutes, stirring every so often, until the rice is tender. Remove from the heat and leave the rice to stand, covered, for 15–20 minutes before serving.

This recipe uses the stock from the lamb to cook the rice for extra meaty goodness.

GRANAT SOUP

SERVES: **4**

PREP: **20 MINUTES**

COOK: **1 HOUR**

8 chicken thighs

1 tbsp All Purpose Seasoning

8 spring onions, finely sliced

2 tbsp vegetable oil

1 onion, diced

2 garlic cloves, sliced

2.5cm piece fresh root ginger, peeled and grated

200g tomatoes, diced

2 bay leaves

3 tbsp tomato paste

340g smooth peanut butter

1–2 Scotch bonnet chillies, depending on how hot you like it, pricked

4 Maggi or other vegetable stock cubes

salt and black pepper, to taste

TO SERVE:

handful of peanuts

handful of coriander, roughly chopped

4–6 spring onions, sliced

Peanut butter and soup, doesn't that just sound mad? Peanut butter is a classic ingredient in Sierra Leonean cooking, mainly used in stews, but we also just love the peanut in general. You will always see someone on the streets of Freetown yamming away on a bag of peanuts while enjoying a conversation with a friend. The lovely earthy flavour from the nutty spread is something that, once tried in a stew, instead of a PBJ, will make you see how interesting West African cooking really is.

Add the chicken thighs to a saucepan and cover with 800ml water, then stir in the All Purpose Seasoning and half the spring onions. Bring to the boil and simmer for 30 minutes.

Meanwhile in a large saucepan, add the oil and brown the onion over a medium heat for 10 minutes before adding the garlic and ginger. Fry until fragrant, then add the tomatoes and the rest of the spring onions and cook for a further 5 minutes. Add the bay leaves and tomato paste and cook for 1 minute or so. Finally, stir in the peanut butter, Scotch bonnets and stock cubes, season and stir well to combine.

Add the cooked chicken and 600ml of the stock from the chicken pan. Simmer for 15–20 minutes until thickened, then serve topped with the peanuts, coriander and spring onions.

Crush the garlic with a fork like Zuu's mum.

UNLIMITED PERI CHICKEN

SERVES: **4**

PREP: **15 MINUTES**

MARINADE: **6+ HOURS**

COOK: **45 MINUTES**

1 large chicken (about 1.8kg)

FOR THE MARINADE:

12 peri-peri or bird's-eye chillies

12 dried peri-peri chillies

5 garlic cloves

3 tbsp dried oregano

3 tbsp paprika

160ml olive oil

120ml red wine vinegar

4 tbsp brown sugar

2 tsp salt

I worked at Nando's, so this one is emotional for me. I was a griller, so if you dined at Nando's on Berners Street, central London, during 2013–2014, chances are I cooked your chicken. Peri-peri is such a great way to use spice for its variation in flavour rather than just its heat. Bird's-eye chillies really do make the difference, so if you can get your hands on them, do, because that's what gives this dish its authentic taste. Can't believe I just said that by the way. I sound like Jamie Oliver.

Place all the marinade ingredients together in a blender and blend until smooth. Rub about two-thirds of the marinade all over the chicken and chill in the fridge for 6–12 hours. When you are ready to cook, remove from the fridge about 30 minutes before cooking and allow the chicken to come to room temperature.

Preheat the oven to 240°C/220°C fan/Gas 9.

To spatchcock the chicken, turn the bird over on a board so the breasts are facing down. The chicken's backbone runs down the middle. Using a pair of kitchen scissors, cut down either side of the backbone to remove it entirely. (Save this for making stock.) Flip the chicken back over to be breast-side up and firmly push down in the middle of the breast bone to flatten it. Your chicken is spatchcocked!

Place the chicken in a tray lined with foil and roast for 45 minutes – the skin will be blistered and charred like a good barbecued chicken. To check if the chicken is cooked through, insert a skewer through a thigh – the juices should run clear. Remove from the oven and rest for 15 minutes.

In a pan, simmer the remaining marinade with the juices from the tray the chicken cooked in for 5 minutes for an intense peri-peri gravy, or simply serve the uncooked marinade alongside the chicken – it works both ways!

BOSSMAN CHICKEN SHAWARMA

SERVES: **4**

PREP: **15 MINUTES**

MARINADE: **2+ HOURS**

COOK: **30 MINUTES**

800g boneless skinless chicken thighs

2 tbsp vegetable oil

FOR THE MARINADE:

1 tbsp ground cumin

1 tbsp ground coriander

1 tsp paprika

¼ tsp ground cardamom

1 tsp dried thyme

1 tsp garlic powder

1 tsp baharat

½ tsp cayenne pepper

1 tsp salt

2 tbsp white vinegar

TO SERVE:

4 flatbreads, warmed

Lebanese pickles and pickled chillies

2 tomatoes, sliced

1 cos lettuce, shredded

1 small red onion, finely sliced

½ cucumber, sliced

yoghurt or hummus

How do you make a beautiful Lebanese shawarma at home without bringing your local bossman to your house and having the massive machine that spins the kebab, plus a salad station, and enough chilli and garlic sauce to fill your bathtub? Well, here is a simple way to enjoy a kebab at home without feeling guilty about what's in it. Basically, you don't need to be drunk to enjoy this kebab.

Lay each chicken thigh out flat and cut in half to make 2 roughly square pieces. Mix together all the marinade ingredients in bowl, then rub all over the chicken pieces. Cover and marinate in the fridge for at least 2 hours.

Preheat the oven to 220°C/200°C fan/Gas 7 and preheat a griddle over a medium heat.

Take a chicken piece and pierce with a 25cm-long metal skewer at each end so that the chicken is stretched between the two skewers. Repeat with all the chicken pieces, squeezing them tightly together on the skewers to make a densely packed kebab.

Brush the kebab all over with the vegetable oil and lay carefully on the griddle. Grill on one side for 4–5 minutes until golden brown or even lightly charred. Turn and repeat on all sides. When the shawarma has been grilled all over, transfer to a foil-lined oven tray and cover with foil. Place in the oven and roast for 20 minutes to cook the centre of the shawarma.

Rest the shawarma for 5 minutes before serving with the flatbreads, pickles, vegetables, yoghurt or hummus.

Don't use oil in the shawarma marinade as it will stop the chicken holding together and staying moist while cooking.

MOROCCAN CHICKEN BASTILLA

2 tbsp olive oil

650g boneless skinless chicken thighs, halved

1 onion, sliced

4 garlic cloves, sliced

1 tsp turmeric

2 tsp ground cumin

1 tsp ground ginger

½ tsp saffron

1 tbsp warm water

large handful of parsley, finely chopped

large handful of coriander, finely chopped

350ml chicken stock

1 tsp salt

4 eggs, beaten

2 tbsp icing sugar, plus extra to dust

½ tsp ground black pepper

75g flaked almonds, lightly toasted

½ tsp ground cinnamon

250g packet filo pastry

100g butter, melted

Never thought I would be able to harness the skill needed to create this sweet but savoury piece of food that I've had so many times at the houses of my Moroccan friends. But trust me, this is a very lovely thing that has so many layers of flavour it will make you feel like you're in Marrakesh, riding a camel with your babes.

In a large saucepan, heat the oil, then brown the chicken pieces on all sides before removing from the pan and setting aside. Add the onion and garlic to the pan and cook together over a medium heat for 10 minutes until golden, then add the turmeric, cumin and ginger.

Crush the saffron in a pestle and mortar or with the back of a spoon in a bowl and mix with the warm water. Leave to stand for 5 minutes, then add to the pan and stir well. Mix in the parsley and coriander, then return the chicken to the pan with the chicken stock and salt. Simmer gently for 25 minutes until the chicken is cooked through.

Remove the chicken pieces and set aside. Bring the stock remaining in the pan to the boil. Add the beaten eggs, half the icing sugar and the pepper and scramble the eggs quickly in the pan – they will soak up the remaining liquid. Remove from the heat and transfer to a bowl. Shred the cooked chicken and mix with the egg mixture. Leave to cool completely.

Preheat the oven to 210°C/190°C fan/Gas 6½.

In a food processor, pulse the toasted almonds with the rest of the icing sugar and cinnamon until the mixture resembles breadcrumbs.

Grease a 20cm round springform tin with vegetable oil. Remove the filo sheets from the fridge and keep covered with a damp tea towel while you assemble the pie.

Brush a sheet of filo with melted butter, then place into the tin, allowing an overlap on either side. Repeat this with 2 more sheets of filo, changing the position of the sheets each time so that the overlap covers all sides of the tin. Sprinkle in 2 tablespoons of the almond mixture, then lay in 3 more sheets of buttered filo, overlapping each time. Then spoon in the cooled chicken mixture.

Fold the overlap from the bottom sheets over the chicken, tucking in the mix. Cover with 3 more buttered sheets of filo, tucking in slightly around the edges. Sprinkle over the remaining almond mixture. Butter the remaining 3 sheets of filo. Fold the overlap from the top 3 sheets back onto the pie, then take the remaining buttered filo sheets and scrunch gently before pressing onto the top to make a lovely textured lid.

Bake in the oven for 1 hour until the pie is golden brown. Leave to stand for 10 minutes before removing from the tin, dusting with more icing sugar and serving.

JERK CHICKEN

SERVES: **4**

PREP: **20 MINUTES**

MARINADE: **3+ HOURS**

COOK: **45 MINUTES**

1kg chicken (thighs and drumsticks on the bone)

2 tbsp vegetable oil

FOR THE JERK DRY RUB:

1 tbsp ground allspice

1 tsp salt

1 tbsp All Purpose Seasoning

1 tsp garlic powder

1 tsp onion powder

1 tsp ground ginger

3 tsp dried thyme

½ tsp white pepper

1 tsp sugar

½ tsp ground cinnamon

FOR THE JERK WET RUB:

2 Scotch bonnet chillies

4 garlic cloves

5cm piece fresh root ginger, peeled and roughly chopped

4 spring onions

2 tbsp white vinegar

1 tbsp thyme leaves

1 tsp ground allspice

Proper jerk chicken is not easy to get right at home, but don't worry, me, Tubsey and Hyder have eaten so much jerk that we can confirm this recipe is definitely good enough for you lot to enjoy in your yard when you are trying to tap into your inner yard man. This doesn't have to be done with just chicken though – you can use different meats, seafood or even vegetables in the same way to bring some island vibes to your cheffing.

Combine all the jerk dry rub ingredients together. You don't need all of it for this recipe, but can store this in a jar for 1 month.

Rub 3 tablespoons of the dry rub all over the chicken pieces, cover and leave to marinate in the fridge for at least 1 hour.

In a food processor, blend together all the jerk wet rub ingredients.

Remove the chicken from the fridge and smother in the wet rub – wear gloves as the Scotches will really get under your skin. Return the chicken to the fridge to marinate for a further 2 hours.

You can barbecue the jerk chicken, but if you don't have the option at home, then use this method for similar results:

Preheat the oven to 240 C/220°C fan/Gas 9. Spread the chicken pieces on a foil-lined roasting tray, skin-side up. Drizzle a bit of the oil on the skin of each chicken piece, then place in the oven on a high shelf for 45 minutes. Remove from the oven, rest for 10 minutes and serve with Rice 'n' Peas (see page 154).

Use the leftover jerk dry rub to spice up scrambled eggs, mix with butter and crushed garlic to make jerk garlic bread or use it like AJ Tracey to make the Live & Direct Mince (see page 101).

ALI'S ZERESHK POLO (IRANIAN CHICKEN)

SERVES: **6**

PREP: **20 MINUTES**

COOK: **1 HOUR**

2 tbsp olive oil

1kg chicken thighs and drumsticks

1 onion, sliced

2 garlic cloves, sliced

½ tsp turmeric

½ tsp ground cumin

½ tsp ground cardamom

2 tbsp tomato paste

1 tsp saffron, crushed and soaked in 4 tbsp warm water

2 tomatoes, diced

400ml chicken stock

400g basmati rice, washed and soaked for 30 minutes

50g butter or ghee

30g barberries

salt

Big up my brudda Ali, whose house I would always go to and have home-cooked Iranian food. This dish was just a lil' chicken stew to his family, but for me it was an amazing dinner! The sweet and sour flavours in the stew were so different to the cooking I was used to, and from this dish I saw how beautiful Persian cuisine is. I'm so happy my broski Ali was able to get this authentic recipe from his mum for me to share with you.

Heat the oil in a large frying pan and brown the chicken pieces over a medium heat. When the chicken is nicely browned all over, set aside and add the onion to the pan. Fry for 10 minutes, then add the garlic and ground spices. Stir in the tomato paste and 2 tablespoons of the saffron water and cook for 2 minutes before adding the tomatoes. Add the chicken back into the pan, season well with salt and pour in the chicken stock. Simmer gently on a low heat for 45 minutes.

Meanwhile, bring a large pan of salted water to the boil. Add the rice and boil for 7 minutes before draining and rinsing under cold water. Add 1 tablespoon of butter of ghee or to a non-stick saucepan with a tight-fitting lid and then pile in the rice. Make some holes through the rice layer using a chopstick, then cover with a tea towel and the lid. Place over a low heat to steam for 20 minutes.

Heat the remaining butter or ghee in a small pan, then add the barberries. Fry the barberries for 2 minutes, then add the remaining saffron water.

Remove the rice from the heat. Mix 3 or 4 big spoonfuls of rice in a bowl with the saffron and barberry mixture. Turn out the remaining rice onto a large plate and top with the saffron rice. Serve with the chicken.

Crushing the saffron and mixing it with warm water makes it go further and really permeate the dish.

ALI'S HAVIJ POLO
(CARROT & SHREDDED CHICKEN RICE)

SERVES: **6**

PREP: **20 MINUTES**

COOK: **1¼ HOURS**

2 tbsp olive oil

1 tbsp butter

250g carrots, peeled and sliced into thin strips

1 onion, finely sliced

½ tsp turmeric

½ tsp salt

1 tsp caster sugar

300g cooked shredded chicken

400g basmati rice, rinsed and soaked for 30 minutes

½ tsp saffron, crushed and mixed with 2 tbsp warm water

2 tbsp ghee

My brudda Ali Katal is back with another Iranian classic. This one makes the all-time top three ways to use a carrot. Again, big blessings to his mum for gracing us with this recipe for the people to experience. Persian food is normally seen as kebabs and rice, but this dish is a homage to the unique ways veg and meat are prepared that you will never see, except in the land of Iran.

Heat the oil and butter in a pan and add the carrots and onion. Fry over a medium heat for 10–15 minutes until golden and soft before adding the turmeric, salt and sugar. Mix with the cooked shredded chicken and set aside.

Bring a large pan of well-salted water to the boil. Add the soaked rice and boil for 5 minutes before draining and rinsing in cold water. Season well. Place two-thirds of the rice in a bowl and mix in the saffron water.

Heat the ghee in a non-stick frying pan with a tight-fitting lid. Add half the saffron rice, then top with half the chicken mixture. Follow with the white rice, then the rest of the chicken mixture. Top with the remaining saffron rice and cover with a tea towel and the lid – make sure the towel isn't close to the heat. Leave over a low heat to steam for 50 minutes.

Remove from the heat and carefully turn out onto a plate. Serve immediately.

CHICKEN TERIYAKI JYU

SERVES: **2**

PREP: **30 MINUTES**

COOK: **30 MINUTES**

80ml soy sauce

80ml sake or rice vinegar

3 tbsp sugar

4 boneless chicken thighs, about 500g

300g sushi rice, washed

2 tbsp vegetable oil

80g cos or your favourite lettuce, roughly chopped

2 tomatoes, quartered

½ small red onion, finely sliced

2 tbsp Japanese-style mayonnaise (e.g. Kewpie) or salad cream

2 spring onions, shredded

FOR THE DRESSING:

2.5cm piece fresh root ginger, peeled and grated

1 tsp soy sauce

1 tsp Dijon mustard

2 tsp rice wine vinegar

4 tbsp neutral oil, such as vegetable or sunflower

Eat Tokyo is a restaurant Tubsey, Hyder and I used to all deliver food from when we worked for Uber Eats. If it wasn't for that, we probably would have never had this dish, and our only understanding of chicken teriyaki would have been the one we got at Subway. I order this all the time when I'm at the studio, so being able to make it at home is a great feeling 'cause it's cheaper and you can put your own spin on it.

Combine the soy, sake or rice vinegar and sugar in a bowl and mix well. Cover the chicken thighs in the marinade, cover and leave at room temperature for 30 minutes.

Meanwhile, in a saucepan bring the sushi rice and 400ml cold water to the boil. When the rice comes to the boil, put on a tight lid and leave to simmer for 15 minutes over a low heat. Remove the rice from the heat but leave the lid on to steam for a further 15 minutes.

To make the salad dressing, whisk together the ginger, soy, mustard and vinegar in a jug. Then slowly whisk in the oil until you get a thick dressing. Set aside.

Remove the chicken from the marinade and set aside. Pour the marinade into a small saucepan and bring to the boil. Cook until reduced by half.

Meanwhile, heat the oil in a large frying pan over a medium heat. Place the chicken thighs flat in the pan and cover with a piece of baking parchment, then place a heavy pan or tray on top to flatten the chicken completely. Fry slowly for 4–5 minutes, then turn over, flatten again and cook for a further 5 minutes.

To assemble, dress the lettuce, tomatoes and red onion with the gingery dressing. Fluff the rice with a fork and spoon onto two plates. Slice the chicken and place on top of the rice, then brush all over with the sticky reduced sauce. Garnish with the salad, then drizzle with the mayo or salad cream. Top with shredded spring onions and serve.

This teriyaki marinade works so well with salmon, tuna, prawns, beef, tofu, anything.

THE BIG DARG DOG

MAKES: **2**

PREP: **15 MINUTES**

COOK: **40 MINUTES**

3 tbsp vegetable oil

2 onions, finely sliced

2 rashers of turkey bacon, diced

2 hot dog rolls

100g cream cheese

1 tbsp sriracha

½ tsp smoked paprika

2 beef hot dogs

handful of pickled jalapeños

American mustard, for drizzling

dollop of soured cream

handful of onion Kettle chips

Hot dogs or cold cats? You decide. This is a bad boy way to create a hot dog and involves a lot of things that sound weird, but actually lead to full-time joy. Like when Liverpool won the Champions League and I was there in Madrid, just had to throw that in. Up the Reds, YNWA.

Heat 2 tablespoons of the oil in a frying pan, then add the onions. Gently fry over a low-medium heat for 15 minutes until the onions are starting to caramelise, then add the bacon. Continue to fry the bacon and onions together for another 15 minutes until the onion and bacon bits are caramelised and delicious. Remove from the pan but reserve any oil in the pan. Set aside.

Slice the middle of the hot dog rolls nearly the whole way through so they are still intact. Toast the cut sides of the rolls in the residual oil from the onions and bacon until they are just golden and crisp. Set aside.

In a bowl, combine the cream cheese with the sriracha and smoked paprika.

Finally, heat the remaining 1 tablespoon of oil in the pan and fry the hot dogs over a medium heat on all sides until evenly brown and crisp.

Assemble the dogs by spreading the inside of each roll with the cream cheese mixture. Stuff a hot dog in each roll, then top with the caramelised onions and bacon, jalapeños, a drizzle of mustard and finally crumble over some Kettle chips for a crispy finish.

Don't waste the leftover oil from the onions and bacon! Use it to toast the buns for a deeper flavour.

BIG ZUU BOLOGNESE

SERVES: **4–6**

PREP: **15 MINUTES**

COOK: **1½ HOURS**

2 tbsp olive oil

60g salted butter

1 onion, diced

500g beef mince

4 garlic cloves, crushed

2 tsp paprika

½ tsp chilli powder

2 tbsp tomato paste

2 x 400g tins chopped tomatoes

1 tbsp brown sugar

1 tbsp soy sauce

1 tbsp All Purpose Seasoning

2 tbsp whole milk

200ml beef stock

1 Parmesan or hard cheese rind hanging around at the back of the fridge (optional)

500g spaghetti

Mumma Zuu used to make this for me all the time and it's lovely because the more cooking I've done, the more ways I've learnt to make this dish even better. So many people have their version of a spag bol, but this recipe has been tried and tested on many of my friends, and they can confirm the peng level. So if you don't believe me, give them a DM on Insta and see for yourself.

In a large saucepan, heat the oil and half the butter together (put the rest of the butter in the fridge to keep cold) and fry the onion over a medium heat for about 15 minutes until golden and softened. Add the mince, breaking it up with a wooden spoon, and fry until completely browned and the liquid has evaporated.

Add the garlic, paprika and chilli powder and cook for 2 minutes before adding the tomato paste. Fry for a further 2 minutes, then add the tomatoes, sugar, soy sauce and All Purpose Seasoning. Stir in the milk, stock and the cheese rind, if using. Leave to simmer gently for 1 hour.

When the sauce is almost ready, cook the spaghetti according to the packet instructions. To serve, drain the spaghetti, reserving some pasta water, and toss in the hot meat sauce with the rest of the cold butter stirred through and a little pasta water to loosen. Serve immediately.

Adding your old Parmesan or other hard cheese rinds to the sauce gives it a huge umami kick. Also, adding a couple of tablespoons of milk counteracts any bitterness in the tomatoes and gives the sauce richness.

THE OG LASAGNE

SERVES: **4–6**

PREP: **30 MINUTES**

COOK: **1¾ HOURS**

30g butter

700ml whole milk

30g plain flour

100g Cheddar, grated

100g Red Leicester, grated

30g Parmesan, grated

1 tsp Dijon mustard

1 tsp hot sauce

100ml single cream

1 quantity of Big Zuu Bolognese (see page 79)

15 lasagne sheets (about 250–300g)

125g mozzarella

1 shop-bought garlic baguette

1 tablespoon olive oil

large handful of parsley, finely chopped

My brudda Alhan loves clowning me on the fact that I can only cook lasagne. This was my go-to dish when people asked me if I could cook because it required the return of The Roux Lord and my beautiful Bolognese recipe, so it was a no-brainer. The best lasagne is served set and warm, so make sure you leave time for this one because there is nothing worse than a sloppy lasagne that isn't set properly – what was the point in all that effort of layering?

To make the cheese sauce, melt the butter in a large saucepan over a medium heat. Heat the milk in another saucepan. When the butter has melted and is just foaming, whisk in the flour. Cook the roux for 2 minutes before whisking in a ladleful of the warm milk. Once that is completely combined, whisk in another ladleful and whisk until completely combined. Repeat until all the milk is used. Simmer the sauce for 1–2 minutes, then take off the heat. Whisk in just over half the Cheddar and Red Leicester and two-thirds of the Parmesan, then whisk in the mustard, hot sauce and cream.

Preheat the oven to 200°C/180°C fan/Gas 6.

Heat the Bolognese sauce in the microwave or on the hob and use any oil from the top of it to grease the bottom of a 25 x 30cm ovenproof dish. Spread a layer of Bolognese on the bottom of the dish, then spread a ladleful of the cheese sauce. Cover with a layer of lasagne sheets and repeat with another layer each of Bolognese and cheese sauce. Sprinkle over half the remaining Cheddar, Red Leicester and Parmesan and top with half the mozzarella. Repeat with another layering of the meat sauce, cheese sauce and pasta. Top the final pasta layer with the remaining cheeses, scattering them evenly over the surface.

Cover with foil and bake for 45 minutes. At the same time, bake the garlic baguette according to the packet instructions.

When the garlic baguette is cooked, remove from the oven and leave to cool before chopping into small pieces. Toss the garlic bread pieces with the oil and parsley.

After the lasagne has had its 45 minutes, remove the foil. Cover the top with the chopped garlic baguette and return to the oven, uncovered, for 15–20 minutes until golden brown. Remove from the oven and leave to stand for 20 minutes before serving.

BUN THE PIZZA OVEN PIZZA

FOR THE DOUGH:

275ml warm water

1 tbsp extra-virgin olive oil

1 tbsp brown sugar

7g sachet fast-action yeast

450g strong bread flour,
plus extra for dusting

1 tsp salt

FOR THE PIZZA SAUCE:

2 tbsp extra-virgin olive oil

2 garlic cloves, crushed

400g passata

1 tbsp dried oregano

1 tsp dried basil

1 tsp caster sugar

salt and ground black
pepper, to taste

Making a pizza at home is always a long concept and home delivery has definitely taken over, so here is an easy way for you to galvanise your love for pizza and experiment with toppings on a simple base that you can make at home. We all love pizza, but some people can't take in the cheese or the gluten (get a new belly) so you can always remix this to make it work for you – inclusivity, always, on *Big Zuu's Big Eats*.

To make the dough, add the warm water, oil, sugar and yeast to a jug, mix well together and set aside for 5 minutes – it should have a few bubbles and become cloudy.

In a large bowl, mix the flour and salt together and make a well in the middle. Pour in the yeast mixture. Use a fork to mix the wet into the dry and when the mixture starts pulling away from the sides use your hands to bring it together into a dough.

Transfer onto a lightly floured surface and knead for 5 minutes until smooth. Move the dough to a clean, lightly oiled bowl and cover with an oiled piece of clingfilm. Leave to prove in a warm place for 2 hours.

Meanwhile, make the sauce by heating the oil in a saucepan over a medium heat. Add the garlic and fry for 1–2 minutes until just going golden before adding the passata, oregano, basil and sugar. Bring to a simmer and cook over a low heat for 25 minutes. Season and set aside.

When the dough has proved for 2 hours, preheat the oven to 245°C/225°C fan/Gas 9.

Turn the dough out onto a lightly floured surface and knead lightly. Roll the dough into a cylinder shape and divide this into 4 equal pieces. Shape the pieces into balls, then place on an oiled baking sheet. Cover with another baking sheet and leave to prove for 20 minutes while you prep your pizza toppings and the oven gets hot.

FOR A MARGARITA PIZZA:

3 tbsp Pizza Sauce

60g mozzarella

1 tsp dried oregano

basil leaves

1 tbsp extra-virgin olive oil, for drizzling

FOR A ZUU SPECIAL:

3 tbsp Pizza Sauce

70g cooked chicken

2 tbsp tinned sweetcorn, drained

60g mozzarella or smoked mozzarella

1 green chilli, sliced

1 tsp dried oregano

basil leaves

1 tbsp extra-virgin olive oil, for drizzling

When you are ready to cook, place a 25cm frying pan over a medium heat.

Place one dough ball on a lightly floured surface and stretch it into a rough circle about the same size as the bottom of the pan - about 22cm. Try to aim for a thick crust and a thin centre. Carefully place the dough into the pan, stretching out the sides to the very edge of the pan. Leave to cook gently for 5-6 minutes, by which time the central thinner part will have dried out a bit. Then add your toppings.

If your frying pan has an ovenproof handle, put it straight into the oven. If not, transfer the pizza to an oven tray (this should be easy as the base is part-cooked at this point). Place in the hot oven and cook for 11-12 minutes for a super-crispy, delicious base and hot melted cheese. Finish with a drizzle of oil. Repeat to make the other three pizzas.

Make a garlic butter, mix with some grated mozzarella and use this to make an incredible cheesy garlic bread.

SUPERMALT SHORT RIBS

SERVES: **4–6**

PREP: **15 MINUTES**

MARINADE: **2+ HOURS**

COOK: **6 HOURS**

1.5kg beef short ribs

2 tbsp vegetable oil

2 large onions, sliced

2 garlic cloves, crushed

2.5cm piece fresh root ginger, peeled and grated

1 Scotch bonnet chilli, pierced

2 x 330ml bottles Supermalt

4 Maggi or other vegetable stock cubes

1 tbsp tomato ketchup

1 tbsp honey

coleslaw and other sides, to serve

FOR THE DRY RUB:

2 tbsp All Purpose Seasoning

1 tsp garlic powder

1 tsp dried thyme

1 tbsp ground cumin

1 tsp fine salt

Even if you don't like malt beer, please don't be a hater – this is so buff. We are definitely the first people to put out this recipe, even though we cannot legally own it. So, when you make this, I beg you, remember who showed you the ways, my G, 'cause this right here is innovation at its finest. Most of the time we don't eat ribs 'cause they are pretty much always pork, so this one is for my Akhis and Ukhtis.

Mix all the ingredients for the dry rub together in a bowl and rub all over the ribs. Cover and marinate in the fridge for at least 2 hours and up to 12 hours.

Preheat the oven to 170°C/150°C fan/Gas 3½.

In a large casserole, heat the oil over a medium heat. Add the onions and cook, stirring often, for 15 minutes until browned and soft. Add the garlic and ginger and fry for 2 minutes before adding the Scotch bonnet, Supermalt and 200ml water. Add the stock cubes and bring to the boil.

Place the marinated ribs in a large, deep roasting tray or ceramic or glass dish lined with foil, then pour over the malt beer and onion stock. Cover the tray or dish with foil and place in the oven to cook for 5–5 ½ hours until the ribs are super-tender, checking and turning them a couple of times during cooking.

Remove the ribs from the liquid and set them aside on a foil-lined tray, covering with foil to keep warm. Turn the oven up to 245°C /225°C fan/Gas 9.

Strain the cooking liquid into a saucepan, pushing the oniony juices through the sieve as much as possible. Place over a high heat. Bring the liquid to the boil, whisk in the ketchup and honey and cook until reduced by half and thickened.

Pour the thickened sauce over the short ribs and put back into the oven, uncovered, for 10 minutes to glaze. Serve immediately with coleslaw, your favourite sides and a cold bottle of Supermalt.

ALBONDIGAS SUB
(SPANISH MEATBALL)

SERVES: **2**

PREP: **20 MINUTES**

COOK: **15 MINUTES**

250g beef mince

20g white breadcrumbs

1 tbsp shop-bought crispy onions, crushed

1 tsp smoked paprika

2 garlic cloves, grated

20g Manchego cheese, grated

handful of finely chopped parsley

TO SERVE:

1 quantity of Garlic Aïoli (see page 167)

2 medium baguettes or submarine rolls, halved lengthways

2 tbsp pitted green olives, roughly chopped

2 piquillo peppers, sliced

½ quantity of Bravas Sauce (see page 116), warmed

125 mozzarella, sliced

20g Manchego cheese, sliced

Thank you to my Spanish bae and her family for this one. I love a sandwich, and this is a lovely way to bring Subway to your yard with some Español essence. A different spin on the meatball, which I think is sick because, instead of going with a classic Italian, we flipped it, which is the ethos of *Big Eats* cooking, and a great way to introduce new cuisines to your repertoire.

Preheat the oven to 245°C/225°C fan/Gas 9.

To make the meatballs, mix all the ingredients well together in a bowl, then shape into 8 walnut-sized balls. Place on a foil-lined tray and cook in the oven for 12 minutes.

Switch the oven to grill on high.

To assemble a sub, spread half the Äioli on the bottom of half of 1 baguette or roll, then top with half the olives and peppers and some Bravas Sauce. Arrange 4 meatballs on top and drizzle with more of the Bravas Sauce. Cover with half the mozzarella and Manchego. Repeat for the second sub.

Place the subs on a foil-lined tray with their lids cut-side up next to them, then grill until the cheese is melted and the bread lid is nicely toasted. Squish the lids on top and serve immediately.

Use crispy onions in the meatball mix for low-effort flavour!

BIG ZUU'S TRAP BOX

SERVES: **4**

PREP: **2 HOURS**

MARINATE: **2+ HOURS**

COOK: **1 HOUR**

FOR THE SUYA LAMB RIBS:

1 tsp garlic powder

1 tsp ground ginger

1 tsp hot chilli powder

1 tsp paprika

1 tsp fine salt

3 Maggi or other vegetable stock cubes, crushed

¼ tsp white pepper

60g peanuts, finely chopped

800g lamb ribs

FOR THE SWEET CHILLI CHICKEN NUGGETS:

1 quantity of ZFC Brine (see page 20)

500g chicken tenders

1.5l vegetable oil, for deep-frying (if using a saucepan; if using a deep-fat fryer follow manufacturer's instructions for oil)

50g plain flour

25g cornflour

25g rice flour

200ml sweet chilli sauce

If you haven't seen a trap box on Instagram you probably don't follow the right people. This is what peng food looks like, my friend – all the maddest, most moreish, magical dishes come together like *The Avengers* in a food takeover that would've defeated Thanos in the first film. Big up Trap Kitchen and Biggz Soul Food for the inspiration.

To make the suya lamb, mix the garlic, spices, salt, stock cubes, pepper and peanuts together in a bowl, then rub all over the lamb ribs. Cover and leave to marinate in the fridge for a minimum of 2 hours and up to 12 hours.

Brine the chicken nuggets following the recipe on page 20, cover and leave in the fridge for at least 2 hours and up to 6 hours.

Preheat the oven to 245°C/225°C fan/Gas 9.

To make the Cajun butter, beat together the butter, chilli, garlic, spices and Old Bay-style seasoning until well combined.

Prep the lobster tails by using kitchen scissors to cut through the top of the shell. Cut to about halfway down the tail, just opening it up and exposing the meat - do not cut all the way through. Insert a skewer lengthways down each tail and chill until needed.

For the corn on the cob, rub each well in butter and dust with the Old Bay-style seasoning before wrapping in foil.

Make the mac 'n' cheese according to the recipe on page 149 and set aside to grill later.

Lay the lamb ribs out on a foil-lined tray. Place in the oven on a high shelf and roast for 25 minutes, turning once. At the same time, place the corn in the oven and cook for 30 minutes.

Meanwhile, heat a griddle pan over a medium heat. Preheat the oil in a deep-fat fryer to 165°C or heat the oil in a deep saucepan over a medium-high heat to 165°C.

Ingredients and method continued overleaf →

FOR THE CAJUN GRILLED LOBSTER:

100g salted butter, softened

1 red chilli, finely chopped

4 garlic cloves, crushed

1 tsp paprika

1 tsp Cajun spice

1 tsp Old Bay-style seasoning

4 lobster tails, defrosted if frozen

vegetable oil, for brushing

FOR THE CORN ON THE COB:

2 corns on the cob, halved, or 4 half cobs

50g salted butter, softened

1 tsp Old Bay-style seasoning

FOR THE MAC 'N' CHEESE:

1 quantity of Mac 'n' Cheese by The Roux Lord (see page 149)

FOR THE WAFFLES:

4 shop-bought sweet waffles

40g butter

2 tbsp golden syrup

For the chicken nuggets, mix together the flour, cornflour and rice flour in a bowl. Toss the brined nuggets in the dredge to coat and then carefully lay into the hot oil.

Gently heat the sweet chilli sauce in a saucepan over a low heat. When the chicken nuggets are golden and cooked through, drain on kitchen paper before tossing in the hot sweet chilli sauce. Set aside to keep warm.

Brush the exposed meat of the lobsters with oil. Place on the preheated griddle, meat-side down, for 5 minutes, then transfer to a baking tray, meat-side up. Dollop the Cajun butter over each tail and place in the oven for 6-8 minutes until the butter is melted and the meat just cooked.

Preheat the grill to high. Place the mac 'n' cheese under the grill for 8-10 minutes until bubbling and golden. While this is cooking, heat the waffles in the oven according to the packet instructions.

In a small saucepan, melt together the butter and golden syrup over a gentle heat. Remove the waffles from the oven and brush the melted mixture over the waffles while they are still hot.

Assemble your trap box with the hot ribs, chicken, corn, a serving of mac 'n' cheese, a lobster tail and a waffle each. BOOM.

Skewer the lobster tails so that they don't curl up during cooking.

BEEF 'N' MUSTARD BÁNH MÌ

SERVES: **2**

PREP: **20 MINUTES**

MARINATE: **30 MINUTES**

COOK: **10 MINUTES**

2 red chillies (1 diced, 1 thinly sliced)

1 garlic clove, grated

1 tsp caster sugar

1 tbsp fish sauce

1 tsp rice wine vinegar

1 large sirloin steak (about 250–300g)

1 tbsp vegetable oil

2 small baguettes, split lengthways

2 tbsp mayonnaise

English mustard, for spreading

1 tbsp sriracha

1 small Little Gem lettuce, shredded

½ cucumber, sliced

2 spring onions, sliced

small bunch of mint, torn

small bunch of coriander, torn

small bunch of Thai basil, torn

FOR THE PICKLED VEG:

1 large carrot, peeled and shredded

1 uncooked beetroot, peeled and shredded

100ml warm water

80ml rice wine vinegar

2 tbsp caster sugar

½ tsp salt

1 garlic clove, bashed but left whole

When me and the mandem ate this for the first time, we actually were upset that it wasn't in our lives at an earlier time because it's such a sick concept and tastes like pure joy. A crunchy baguette with lovely beef and that spicy mustard hum. We flipped a classic, but trust me, we did our research. Big up the Bánh Mì Bay, who showed us the authentic turmeric and lemongrass flavour needed in a bánh mì. And big up Rob Delaney for inspiring us to come up with this version that's so great to eat with ya mates.

Mix the diced chilli, garlic, sugar, fish sauce and rice wine vinegar and rub all over the steak to marinate. Set aside for 30 minutes.

To make the pickled vegetables, put the shredded carrot and beetroot in a bowl. In a small jug, mix the warm water with the rice wine vinegar, sugar and salt. Pour over the carrot and beetroot and add the garlic. Leave to pickle for 30 minutes while the steak marinates.

Heat a griddle or frying pan over a high heat. Rub the steak with the oil and cook on a high heat for 2–3 minutes a side for rare or 3–4 minutes a side for medium rare. Leave to rest for 5 minutes, then slice thinly.

Lightly toast the cut side of the baguettes in the griddle or frying pan, then spread with the mayonnaise and some mustard and drizzle with the sriracha. Thinly slice the steak. Fill each baguette with some pickled vegetables, lettuce, cucumber, spring onions, sliced chilli and herbs, then top with the sliced steak and enjoy!

Use the quick pickle marinade for loads of different thinly sliced vegetables – red onions, turnips, cabbage, peppers – whatever you fancy!

ZUU HACKS

THE LEBANESE MIXED GRILL WITH VERMICELLI RICE

FOR THE SHISH TAOUK:

50g natural yoghurt

4 garlic cloves

1 tbsp olive oil

2 tbsp lemon juice

1 tbsp tomato paste

1 tsp paprika

1 tsp dried oregano

½ tsp ground ginger

450g chicken breasts, diced

½ tsp salt

ground black pepper, to taste

FOR THE LAHEM MESHWI:

1 tbsp white vinegar

1 tsp dried oregano

1 tsp dried rosemary

1 tbsp baharat

1 tbsp pomegranate molasses

½ tsp salt

500g lamb leg, diced

ground black pepper, to taste

Would it be a Big Zuu cookbook if we didn't put a mixed grill recipe in there? Come on bro, you know we provide the insight – that all rhymed by the way. No need for Lebanese takeaway, do it at home, fam. The rice is crucial for the real Lebanese experience, so don't slack on the vermicelli please my people, it's defo needed and don't forget your chilli and garlic sauce!

Combine all the ingredients for the shish taouk in a bowl, mixing well. Cover and chill in the fridge at least 2 hours.

To prepare the lahem meshwi, combine the vinegar, oregano, rosemary, baharat, pomegranate molasses and salt and pepper in a bowl. Add the lamb and rub the marinade all over the lamb. Cover and chill in the fridge for at least 2 hours.

For the kafta, combine the lamb with the parsley, onion, spices and salt and pepper in a bowl. Divide the mixture into 4 and shape around 4 metal or soaked wooden skewers. Cover and chill in the fridge for at least 2 hours.

For the vermicelli rice, heat the ghee in a saucepan over a medium heat. Add the vermicelli and toast for 3 minutes in the ghee until just turning a golden brown. Stir in the rinsed and soaked rice, then cover with the boiling water and add the salt. Turn the heat to low, place a tight lid on the pan and steam for 12 minutes. Remove from the heat and allow to steam for 10 more minutes, then stir in the toasted pine nuts and parsley.

FOR THE KAFTA MESHWI:

400g lamb mince

large handful of parsley

½ onion, grated

1 tsp baharat

1 tsp ground cumin

pinch of ground cinnamon

1 tsp ground coriander

1 tsp cayenne pepper

½ tsp salt

ground black pepper, to taste

vegetable oil, for brushing

FOR THE LEBANESE VERMICELLI RICE:

40g ghee

80g egg vermicelli, lightly crushed

300g basmati rice, rinsed and soaked for 30 minutes

600ml boiling water

1 tsp salt

50g toasted pine nuts

handful of parsley, chopped

TO SERVE:

4 good-quality pitta breads

2 tomatoes, sliced

1 cos lettuce, shredded

1 red onion, finely sliced

natural yoghurt

chilli sauce

pickles

Skewer the marinated chicken pieces onto 4 skewers and lamb pieces onto 4 skewers.

Heat a griddle pan over a medium-high heat and start to grill your meats! Brush the kafta with a bit of the oil before grilling. Grill the meats, turning every 2 minutes for about 10-12 minutes.

Preheat the oven to 190°C/170°C fan/Gas 5. Place the pittas on a baking sheet and sprinkle with 2 tablespoons water. Cover tightly with foil and place in the oven for 8-10 minutes until soft and hot.

Set up the garnishes on a plate. Serve the meats with the vermicelli rice, pitta, garnishes and sauces.

Using oil in marinades can sometimes prevent flavour from penetrating the meat – only use it when you are ready to cook!

NO PORK CARBONARA

SERVES: **2**

PREP: **10 MINUTES**

COOK: **15 MINUTES**

2 tbsp olive oil

100g good-quality pastrami, diced

250g spaghetti

3 egg yolks

50g Parmesan or pecorino cheese, plus extra to serve

½ tsp ground black pepper

salt

When you love Italian food as much as I do, it's always so annoying to be unable to enjoy a classic carbonara, but now things are moving different. Big up Vapiano for the inspiration on this one. You lot remembered the Akhis in your restaurant ventures and have secured a customer for life. Enjoy this my people, because Rosie the Pasta Queen worked on this one for me.

In a large frying pan, heat the oil and fry the pastrami over a medium heat for about 10 minutes until crisp.

Meanwhile, bring a large saucepan of salted water to the boil. Add the spaghetti and stir well.

Mix the egg yolks, cheese and pepper together with a pinch of salt in a large bowl.

When the pasta is al dente, scoop out half a mug of pasta water before draining. Add the pastrami and pasta to the egg mixture in the bowl and toss well to combine, adding a splash of pasta water if it is too thick. Serve immediately with more cheese.

THE BOOK OF MEAT & CHEESE

SERVES: **2**

PREP: **20 MINUTES**

COOK: **15 MINUTES**

2 tbsp mayonnaise

1 tbsp American mustard

2 tsp creamed horseradish

2 rib-eye steaks, fat trimmed and reserved

1 onion, finely sliced

1 red pepper, finely sliced

1 green pepper, finely sliced

2 ciabatta rolls, halved

2 tbsp vegetable oil

10 Monterey Jack cheese or Gouda slices

salt and ground black pepper, to taste

Ed Gamble couldn't believe it when we presented him with a sandwich that was basically cheese and steak x 100, but we defo ate all of it so it just proves that this is something you have to make! Bare layers inside is why we called it a book, but if you read this one too much you may stop reading overall, so please try to limit the consumption of this one or maybe lose some layers hahahaha.

Mix the mayonnaise, mustard and horseradish in a bowl, season and set aside.

Melt about 40g of the fat trimmed from the steak slowly in a large frying pan over a medium heat. When the fat has rendered and is coating the pan, fry the onion and peppers for about 8 minutes until they are just charred and softened. Set aside.

In the same pan, lightly toast the ciabatta halves, cut-side down, then spread a thick layer of the horseradish mayo on each half.

Slice the steaks very thinly on the diagonal into 10 pieces each, then, using a rolling pin, beat the pieces to an even thinner width. Season generously with salt and pepper.

Heat the oil in the frying pan (no need to clean it!) until smoking. Carefully lay in the slices of steak and fry for 30 seconds before flipping and covering with the slices of cheese. Cook for another 30 seconds, then take off the heat and cover with a lid – the steam will help to melt the cheese.

To assemble, layer some onion and peppers on the bottom half of each roll, then add a couple of pieces of cheesy steak. Repeat until you have three or four layers of cheesy steak and peppers. Top with the ciabatta lid and serve!

Using the beef fat to cook the peppers and onions gives an even more intense beefy flavour. You could use vegetable oil instead.

AJ TRACEY'S LIVE & DIRECT MINCE

SERVES: **4**

PREP: **15 MINUTES**

COOK: **25 MINUTES**

1 tbsp vegetable oil

1 onion, diced

2 garlic cloves, sliced

1 tsp All Purpose Seasoning

500g beef mince

1 red pepper, diced

1 orange pepper, diced

2 tbsp Jerk Dry Rub
(see page 72)

1 tbsp Jerk Wet Rub
(see page 72)

salt and ground black
pepper, to taste

rice and salad, to serve

TO GARNISH:

1 tomato, diced

2 spring onions, sliced

It's the hyperman set, AJ's mince is live and direct. Hang tight my family AJ Tracey for this recipe. He don't cook a lot, guys, but he defo tried and this, to be fair, is a lovely dish from him. He's made this for me once and that one time was also the only time he's ever cooked for me. I, on the other hand, have cooked for him hundreds of times. Big up my friends though for letting me use them as guinea pigs for my cooking endeavours.

In a large frying pan, heat the oil and fry the onion, garlic and All Purpose Seasoning for 10 minutes over a medium heat. Turn up the heat and add the mince. Fry well, browning the meat and evaporating any liquid.

Add the peppers, Jerk Dry Rub and Jerk Wet Rub and cook for 10-15 minutes until the peppers have softened and the mince is deeply brown and flavourful. Season with salt (but taste first as the Dry Rub contains salt) and pepper. Serve with the rice and salad, then garnish with the tomato and spring onions.

MUMMA ZUU'S OKRA SOUP & FUFU

SERVES: **4**

PREP: **20 MINUTES**

COOK: **1 HOUR 40 MINUTES**

FOR THE OKRA SOUP:

400g stewing beef, diced

3 Maggi or other vegetable stock cubes

2 tbsp All Purpose Seasoning

2 tbsp vegetable oil

2 onions, sliced

4 garlic cloves, sliced

450g tomatoes, diced

2 tbsp tomato paste

1 Scotch bonnet chilli, chopped or pierced, depending on how hot you like it

300g fresh or frozen okra, chopped

salt and ground black pepper, to taste

FOR THE FUFU:

400g cassava or plantain fufu flour

This is my favourite dish of all time. If I was on death row, this is it, this is the plate of food I would want. Not easy to make, but trust me, it is worth all the effort and is one of the best things to come from West Africa, after my mum and using peanut butter in stews. Fufu has a bad rep, but it's actually a great way to get away from your classic pasta and rice. So, if you wanna flip it up at home, give this one a try and you will not regret it. Sierra Leone TO THE WORLD AND BACK! ❤❤❤

Add the stewing beef, 1 stock cube and 1 tablespoon of the All Purpose Seasoning to a saucepan and cover with 800ml water. Bring to the boil and simmer gently for 1 hour, skimming any foam from the stock.

While the meat simmers, heat the oil in a large saucepan and add the onions. Fry for 10 minutes, then add the garlic and tomatoes. Cook for 10 more minutes until the tomatoes have broken down, then add the remaining All Purpose Seasoning and stock cubes, the tomato paste and Scotch bonnet and cook for 2 more minutes.

When the beef has simmered for 1 hour, add it to the stew with its stock. Simmer for another 20 minutes before stirring in the okra and seasoning with salt and pepper. Bring the mixture to the boil and cook for 10 minutes.

To make the fufu, bring 900ml water to a boil in a large saucepan. Slowly mix the fufu flour into the boiling water, adding a little at a time until all the flour is in. Beat the mixture hard with a wooden spoon over a low heat – it will be tough and you need strength! Beat hard for 10 minutes until you have a smooth mixture, adding a little bit of extra water if you need it. Serve immediately with the okra soup.

HYDER'S MUM'S KURDISH DOLMA

800g lamb on the bone (chops and ribs)

1 onion, quartered

1 celery stick, cut into chunks

1 carrot, peeled and cut into chunks

2 bay leaves

3 tbsp vegetable oil

300g lamb mince

4 large onions

4 large tomatoes

4 garlic cloves

small bunch of parsley

small bunch of dill

200g Egyptian or pudding rice, rinsed and soaked for 30 minutes

1 tbsp pomegranate molasses

1 tsp turmeric

juice of 1 lemon

500g leafy Swiss Chard, leaves separated from the stems

2 waxy potatoes, sliced into 1cm rounds

100g frozen broad beans

salt and ground black pepper, to taste

There's never been a dish that represents the Abdullas (aka the Hyder Household) more than this Kurdish Dolma. More sour and juicy than the traditional one you see on a lifeless mezze plate, this particular meal would have me and the lads running to Hyder's house as soon as the news dropped that his mum was soaking the rice. This recipe is a tribute to Hyder's mum, to ensure her dolma lives on and continues to spread the joy we experienced growing up.

Add the lamb pieces to a saucepan along with the onion, celery, carrot and bay leaves. Add 1 teaspoon salt and cover with 800ml water and bring to a simmer. Simmer the lamb for 1 hour, skimming any foam from the stock. Remove the lamb from the stock, cover and set aside.

Meanwhile, to make the rice, heat 1 tablespoon of the oil in a frying pan and fry the lamb mince over a medium heat until well browned, then set aside.

Blend 1 onion, 1 tomato, the garlic, parsley and dill together in a food processor to make a paste.

In a large bowl, mix the paste with the cooked, cooled lamb and the soaked rice. Add the pomegranate molasses, turmeric, 1 teaspoon salt and the lemon juice and set aside.

Make a deep slit down one side, about two-thirds of the way down, of each of the 3 remaining onions so that the core stays intact. Place in a saucepan, cover with water and bring to the boil. Simmer for 10 minutes until the slit has opened wider. Remove from the water and cool under cold running water before peeling away the layers of onion to give you 8–10 onion shells.

Cut a hole in the top of the remaining tomatoes and scoop out the flesh and seeds. Lay the chard leaves out flat. Fill the tomatoes, onion shells and chard leaves with 1 tablespoon each of the rice mixture, wrapping the skins of the onions up and rolling up the chard leaves around the rice.

Heat the remaining oil in a large casserole dish, then lay the sliced potatoes over the base. Season generously with salt and pepper, then start to layer the stuffed leaves and onions, seam-side down, lamb pieces, broad beans, chard stems and stuffed tomatoes, seasoning every layer really well.

Once the pot has everything in it, cover the top layer with a plate that fits in the pot and weigh it down with a tin. Add enough water to just cover, then place over a low heat. Bring to a simmer and cook for 1¼ hours. Leave to stand for 10 minutes before carefully inverting on a rimmed dish and serving.

TUBSEY'S MAI LAHAM & TIMMAN BAGILLA

(LAMB STEW & BROAD BEAN RICE)

SERVES: **4**

PREP: **20 MINUTES**

COOK: **2 HOURS**

FOR THE MAI LAHAM:

2 tbsp olive oil

400g lamb leg, diced

2 onions, sliced

1 tsp turmeric

1 tsp salt

200g dried chickpeas, soaked overnight and drained

1 dried lime, carefully pierced with a knife

FOR THE TIMMAN BAGILLA:

300g basmati rice, rinsed and soaked for 30 minutes

400g frozen peeled broad beans

2 tbsp olive oil

bunch of dill, finely chopped, plus extra to serve

1 tbsp salt

Don't let the name throw you off, this dish isn't as complicated as Tubsey makes cooking look. A classic Iraqi staple that will mean you'll never open your microwaveable rice pouch again, and will make you respect lamb more than Mary. Can't lie, have this one for Sunday lunch and get back to me.

To make the mai laham, heat the oil in a saucepan over a medium heat. Add the lamb pieces and brown all over – do this in batches to prevent overcrowding. Remove the lamb from the pan and set it aside.

Add the onions to the pan and fry for 15 minutes until golden. Add the turmeric, salt, cooked lamb pieces and the chickpeas. Cover everything with 800ml water, add the dried lime and simmer gently for 1½ hours until the lamb and chickpeas are tender.

For the timman bagilla, bring 900ml well-salted water to the boil in a non-stick saucepan. Add the soaked rice and cook for 5 minutes before stirring in the broad beans. Boil for 2 more minutes, then drain well.

Add 1 tablespoon oil to the pan and return the rice and beans to the pan. Stir in the dill and the salt, then cover the pan with a tea towel and tight-fitting lid. Steam the rice over a low heat for 20 minutes. Remove from the heat and fluff with a fork, then add the remaining oil. Serve with the mai laham and more dill.

Rinsing, soaking, boiling and steaming the rice may seem a long process, but it makes the best, most fluffy rice you have ever had.

TUBSEY'S BAMYA
(OKRA STEW)

SERVES: **4**

PREP: **20 MINUTES**

COOK: **1½ HOURS**

600g lamb chops

1 onion, quartered

1 celery stick, cut into chunks

1 carrot, peeled and cut into chunks

2 bay leaves

salt

1 tbsp olive oil

5 garlic cloves, sliced

2 tbsp tomato paste

400g tomatoes, chopped

200g okra

juice of ½ lemon

flatbreads, to serve

How to serve okra ignites many culinary wars across the globe. This is the battle between Ahmed Al Mashayekhi (aka Tubsey) vs Isatu Hamzie (aka Mumma Zuu) for who has the greatest lady finger. This is Tubsey's Iraqi bamya.

Add the chops to a saucepan along with the onion, celery, carrot and bay leaves. Add 1 teaspoon salt, cover with 800ml water and bring to a simmer. Simmer for 1 hour, skimming any foam from the stock.

Meanwhile, in another large saucepan, heat the oil, add the garlic and fry over a medium heat for 1–2 minutes, then add the tomato paste and tomatoes. Cook for 5 minutes.

Remove the lamb from the stock and add to the pan along with 450ml of the lamb stock. Simmer for 20 minutes before adding the whole okra and seasoning with salt. Simmer for another 10 minutes, then add the lemon juice. Serve with flatbreads.

MUMMA ZUU'S PEPPER FISH STEW

SERVES: **4**

PREP: **15 MINUTES**

COOK: **40 MINUTES**

1 onion, diced

2 garlic cloves, sliced

2.5cm piece fresh root ginger, peeled and grated

350g tomatoes, diced

2 tbsp tomato paste

2 Maggi or other vegetable stock cubes

1 tsp cayenne pepper

2 cloves

1 Scotch bonnet chilli, left whole and pierced

4 skinless tilapia fillets (about 500g), each sliced into 4 pieces

salt and ground black pepper, to taste

If you are ill, this is the remedy, trust me. My mum always says it and, if she says it ten million times, it must mean something. A simple way to use fish without just frying or steaming it. This is Africa in a bowl, bare love combined with the rejuvenating elements of humble ingredients that provide life for us and give us the energy to take over the world!

In a large saucepan, bring 1 litre water to the boil, add the onion, garlic and ginger and simmer for 10 minutes. Then add the tomatoes, tomato paste, stock cubes, ½ teaspoon salt, ½ teaspoon pepper, the cayenne pepper, cloves and Scotch bonnet and simmer for 20 minutes until the soup has thickened.

Season the fish well with salt and pepper and add to the soup. Poach the fish in the soup for 8–10 minutes and serve immediately.

JAMAICAN PEPPER SHRIMP

SERVES: **2**

PREP: **10 MINUTES**

COOK: **10 MINUTES**

400g prawns, shells on

2 tbsp olive oil

4 garlic cloves, sliced

4 spring onions, sliced,
plus extra to garnish

1 tbsp thyme leaves

1–2 Scotch bonnet chillies,
depending on how hot you
like it, finely chopped

½ tsp ground black pepper

1 tbsp All Purpose Seasoning

1 tbsp paprika

juice of 2 limes

20g butter

salt

Pepper shrimp is something that, when done correctly, is so finger-licking good it will make you forget KFC existed. Fiery prawns, packed with a punch, can be eaten on their own, but I also love serving them on white rice, to soak up all the juicy drippings. On the barbecue is the best way to cook them, but it also works in a simple pan because the marination is so bloody good!

Devein the prawns by using a sharp knife to slice through the shell to the flesh below and scrape out the black vein – be careful not to go all the way through, it just needs to break the surface. Wash the prawns and drain well.

In a large frying pan heat the oil over a high heat. Add the garlic, spring onions, thyme leaves and Scotch bonnet and fry for 1 minute until fragrant before adding the pepper, All Purpose Seasoning, paprika and half the lime juice.

Cook for 30 seconds, then throw in the prawns and stir well to coat in the spicy mixture. Add the butter and cook, tossing often, for 4–5 minutes until the prawns have all turned a bright pink. Add the remaining lime juice and a pinch of salt before serving.

SARDINES & RICE

SERVES: **1**

PREP: **5 MINUTES**

COOK: **10 MINUTES**

300g cooked rice

20g butter

1 Maggi or other vegetable stock cube, crushed, plus extra for sprinkling

½ tsp chilli powder

½ tsp paprika

1 tsp All Purpose Seasoning

1 tin of sardines, drained

2 spring onions, sliced

salt and ground black pepper, to taste

I grew up very broke, like sardines and rice for dinner broke. If you know about that struggle, big up you. If not, this recipe will make you enjoy something that I used to rely on for dinner but loved so much I didn't see it as a poor man's dish. Very simple and quick to make, also good for you, mate. Come on, what else do you need, what cookbook is throwing it back with struggle meals without violating the mandem?

Heat the rice in a microwave, then mix in the butter, stock cube, chilli powder, paprika, All Purpose Seasoning and some salt and pepper. Top with the sardines and sprinkle over some more stock cube and the spring onions.

Use any tinned fish or tinned meat for a banging cheap meal.

SUMAC SEA BASS & PEPPER SAUCE

SERVES: **2**

PREP: **15 MINUTES**

COOK: **3–4 MINUTES**

2 sea bass fillets
(about 200g)

½ tsp sumac

½ tsp paprika

½ tsp ground cumin

50ml olive oil

100g roasted red peppers
from a jar, finely diced

1 garlic clove, grated

1 tsp dried oregano

handful of parsley, finely
chopped

juice of 1 lemon

1 tbsp vegetable oil

salt and ground black
pepper, to taste

Starting your fish in a cold
pan helps to get your fish
skin super-crisp.

This is such a Hyder dish; he loves fish, and sea bass is like his life. I'm not a fishy guy, but this bangs. The pepper sauce is a bit of shine to my West African roots and our love of spice and fish, always creating a good harmony. The delicate taste of sea bass with the sumac and pepper sauce is a match made in heaven. Trust me on this one.

Dry the sea bass fillets on some kitchen paper, skin-side down. Mix together the sumac, paprika and cumin and sprinkle over the flesh of each fillet.

Combine the olive oil, peppers, garlic, oregano, parsley and half the lemon juice with some salt and pepper in a bowl. Set aside while you cook the fish.

Add the vegetable oil to a cold non-stick pan. Place the sea bass fillets in the pan skin-side down. Then put the pan over a high heat. The skin will cook in the pan as it gets hotter and will become crispy. Keep the fish skin-side down until you can see the skin is a really deep gold and the flesh is halfway to being white – about 3-4 minutes. Then flip the fillets and take the pan off the heat. The flesh will finish cooking in the residual heat and be perfectly cooked.

Serve with the remaining lemon juice and the pepper sauce.

SPANISH VIBES FISH & CHIPS

400g Maris Piper or Désirée potatoes, peeled and cut into roughly 2cm chunks

1.5l vegetable oil, for deep-frying (if using a saucepan; if using a deep-fat fryer follow manufacturer's instructions for oil), plus 120ml vegetable oil for the potatoes

2 cod fillets (about 250–300g)

1 tsp salt

FOR THE BRAVAS SAUCE:

2 tbsp olive oil

1 shallot, finely chopped

3 garlic cloves, sliced

1 red chilli, sliced

2 tsp smoked paprika

300g plum tomatoes, chopped

125g piquillo peppers, chopped

1 tbsp caster sugar

pinch of salt

2 tsp sherry vinegar

We went to Portsmouth and went fishing for this dish, so really I'm now a proper chef as that's what I see them do on TV – go to the source. Wow, I'm basically that old white guy who's always on BBC 2.

Preheat the oven to 200°C /180°C fan/Gas 6.

Put the potatoes in a saucepan of cold, salted water and bring up to the boil. Simmer for 8–10 minutes until cooked, then drain and set aside to cool slightly.

Add the 120ml vegetable oil to an oven tray and toss the potatoes in it, making sure they are all covered well in the oil and are fluffing. Roast cook for 45 minutes, turning every 15 minutes to ensure all sides become golden and crisp.

Place the cod uncovered on a tray and sprinkle over the salt. Return to the fridge for 30 minutes.

Meanwhile, make the bravas sauce. Heat the olive oil in a saucepan, add the shallot and fry gently for 5 minutes until softened. Add the garlic, chilli and paprika and fry for another 2 minutes before adding the tomatoes, peppers, sugar and a pinch of salt. Simmer for 15–20 minutes until the sauce has thickened. Remove from the heat and blend in a food processor until smooth. Add the sherry vinegar, adjust the seasoning if needed and keep warm.

Mix all the ingredients for the aïoli in a bowl and set aside.

Coat the fish in flour, shaking off the excess, then set aside. Whisk together the batter ingredients, then drag the fish through the batter, making sure the fish is completely coated but allowing any excess to drip off.

FOR THE AÏOLI:

100g mayonnaise

1 garlic clove, grated

juice of 1 lemon

FOR THE BATTER:

150g plain flour, plus extra
for dusting

50g cornflour

1 tsp baking powder

pinch of salt

250ml ice-cold lager

10ml ice-cold vodka

TO SERVE:

chopped parsley

lemon wedges

Preheat the oil in deep-fat fryer to 180°C or heat the oil in a deep saucepan over a medium-high heat to 180°C.

Fry the fish for 4-6 minutes (depending on the thickness of the fish) until golden brown, remove and drain on kitchen paper.

Serve the fish with the potatoes drizzled with the bravas sauce and aïoli and sprinkled with the parsley, with lemon wedges on the side. You can add any of your favourite fish and chips sides too!

Salting the cod fillets for 30 minutes draws out any excess moisture and seasons the fish.

VEG & VEGAN

For my veggie dons

JME'S TUK TUK RICE

V-GANG

SERVES: **2**

PREP: **15 MINUTES**

COOK: **15 MINUTES**

2 tbsp vegetable oil

1 red onion, diced

120g Linda McCartney Vegetarian Shredded Hoisin Duck

1 carrot, peeled and diced

1 red pepper, diced

100g tinned sweetcorn, drained

100g frozen peas

250g cooked long grain rice

1–2 tbsp hot sauce, depending on how hot you like it, plus extra to serve

4 tbsp hoisin sauce

TO SERVE:

100g cherry tomatoes, roughly chopped

2 tbsp chia seeds (optional)

2 spring onions, sliced

Jamie (aka JME) is the greatest. I'm honoured he's blessed our book with this special dubplate of a recipe. This is basically an album dedicated to you all. V-Gang forever! Enjoy!

Heat the oil in a large frying pan, then add the onion and vegetarian duck. Cook over a medium heat for 3–4 minutes, stirring regularly. Add the carrot, pepper, sweetcorn and peas and fry for 5 minutes (or you can steam them separately before adding).

Add the rice and stir really well to mix, then add the hot sauce and hoisin sauce. Fry together for a further 5 minutes, ensuring the veggies and rice are all well coated in the hoisin sauce. Serve with a drizzle of hot sauce, the cherry tomatoes, chia seeds, if using, and spring onions.

THE VEGAN DON KEBAB

V-GANG

SERVES: **2**

PREP: **25 MINUTES**

COOK: **20 MINUTES**

1 quantity of Garlic Aïoli (see page 167)

FOR THE FLATBREADS:

100g self-raising flour, plus extra for dusting

½ tsp baking powder

100g plant-based yoghurt (soy or coconut work well)

squeeze of lemon juice

½ tsp salt

FOR THE KEBAB:

1 tsp vegetable oil

200g vegan kebab 'meat', thinly sliced

½ tsp chilli powder

½ tsp dried mint

TO GARNISH:

1 sweet onion, finely sliced

1 tomato, thinly sliced

1 cos lettuce, shredded

¼ small red cabbage, finely shredded

handful of pickled chillies (optional)

hot sauce

This one left Jimmy Carr speechless, which isn't easy – that man can talk for days. This vegan kebab creation (aka The Jimmy Carr-bab) made him fall in love with me and he even proposed we went into business together. So Jimmy, shout me.

For the flatbreads, combine all the ingredients in a large bowl. Turn out onto a clean worktop, knead until smooth, then divide into two. Flour the worktop and roll each piece of dough out as thinly as possible into a large round.

Place a large frying pan or griddle over a medium heat and carefully lay down a flatbread and cook for 2–3 minutes. It should be puffing and slightly charred on the cooked side. Flip and cook for 2–3 minutes on the other side, then transfer to a plate and immediately cover with a clean tea towel (this will keep the flatbread soft). Repeat with the other flatbread.

Heat the oil over a high heat in a large frying pan, add the vegan kebab 'meat', chilli powder and dried mint and fry until the pieces begin to crisp.

Spread each flatbread with a bit of Aïoli and top with the kebab 'meat', vegetables, chillies, if using, hot sauce and any of your favourite kebab-shop sides.

ZUU HACKS

These flatbreads can be used for so many things! Add herbs or spices to the flatbread dough or finish by brushing on garlic butter or grilling with cheese.

PASTA WITH NO JAR TOMATO SAUCE

SERVES: **4**

PREP: **15 MINUTES**

COOK: **1 HOUR**

2 tbsp olive oil

30g salted butter

1 onion, diced

4 garlic cloves, crushed

1 tsp paprika

½ tsp chilli powder

1 tbsp tomato paste

1 tsp dried oregano

1 tbsp brown sugar

1 tbsp soy sauce

1 tsp All Purpose Seasoning

2 x 400g tins chopped tomatoes

500g pasta of your choice

olive oil, to taste

salt and ground black pepper, to taste

your favourite cheese, grated, to serve

I always used ready-made pasta sauce, then I realised cooking down tomatoes with onions and garlic and adding beautiful seasonings is always going to taste better. Trust me, use this sauce and never use a jar again.

In a large saucepan, heat the olive oil and butter together over a medium heat until the butter is just starting to foam. Add the onion and fry gently for 15 minutes until golden. Then add the garlic, paprika and chilli powder and cook for 2 minutes before adding the tomato paste. Cook for 1 minute before adding the oregano, brown sugar, soy sauce, All Purpose Seasoning, the tomatoes and 200ml water. Season with salt and pepper.

Bring up to a simmer and cook for 40 minutes over a low heat until thickened and full of flavour.

Meanwhile, bring a large pan of well-salted water to the boil. Cook the pasta in the boiling water according to the packet instructions and when it is just cooked with a little bite, scoop out some of the pasta water with a mug and drain the pasta.

Combine the cooked pasta with the tomato sauce over the heat, adding a little pasta water to loosen if necessary and some olive oil for extra flavour. Serve immediately topped with your favourite cheese.

This sauce will keep in the fridge for a week – no jar needed.

CACIO E PEPE

120g pasta of your choice

½ tsp freshly ground black pepper

50g butter

60g Parmesan, grated, plus extra to serve

salt

When I went to Rome, I realised we don't really know how to make pasta, but after some in-depth market research (serious eating) I extracted this recipe. It's literally black pepper and cheese mixed with pasta. Doesn't get easier or better than that!

Bring a saucepan of water to the boil and salt generously. Add the pasta, stirring well.

In large frying pan over a low heat, toast the black pepper until fragrant – about 30 seconds. Then add the butter and melt until it is just foaming. Add a small ladleful of the water from the pasta pan and bring to the boil with the butter. Simmer gently while the pasta cooks.

When the pasta is al dente – taste it to check – use a mug to scoop out some of the pasta water before draining. Add the drained pasta straight into the buttery, peppery mix and add the Parmesan. Mix vigorously so that the cheese melts with the butter into a silky smooth sauce. Add splashes of the pasta water that you saved if the sauce is a bit thick. Season with salt and serve with more cheese.

Use tongs or a kitchen spider to move the pasta from the water to the sauce without having to drain it because draining is long.

TOFU LAKSA

V-GANG

400ml vegetable stock

400ml can coconut milk

1 tbsp brown sugar

2 tbsp tamarind paste

1 tbsp soy sauce

250g rice noodles

60g green beans, roughly chopped

3 tofu puffs, halved

100g firm tofu, diced

salt

FOR THE SPICE PASTE:

60ml vegetable oil

1 small shallot, roughly chopped

3 sticks lemongrass, roughly chopped

5cm piece fresh root ginger, peeled and roughly chopped

4 garlic cloves, peeled

2 fresh red chillies

6 dried red chillies, soaked in hot water, or 1 tbsp chilli flakes

2 tsp turmeric powder

2 tsp ground cumin

1 tbsp ground coriander

1 tbsp hot chilli powder

TO SERVE:

handful of coriander

1 red chilli, finely sliced

Not gonna lie, I never knew what a laksa was but, ever since I had one, I think about it every day. Such a punchy broth with crunchy vegetables and silky noodles, this is a bowl of happiness that will take you to Malaysia without having to step on a plane.

In a food processor, blend all the ingredients for the spice paste together until smooth. Add the paste to a large saucepan over a low heat and begin to fry, stirring the paste every so often so it doesn't stick. Cook for 20–30 minutes like this, until the oil starts to separate from the paste.

Add the stock, coconut milk, brown sugar, tamarind paste and soy to the saucepan, season with salt and bring to a boil, then simmer for 15 minutes.

When the soup is ready, cook the rice noodles according to the packet instructions, drain and add to your waiting bowls. Bring a small pan of water to the boil and cook the green beans for 2 minutes before draining and keeping warm. Add the tofu puffs and tofu to the laksa base and simmer for 2 minutes. Build the laksa by ladling the spicy broth over the noodles. Then top with the green beans, tofu puffs and tofu from the broth. Garnish with the coriander and chilli.

GRANDPA KITCHEN'S VEGETABLE BIRYANI

SERVES: **8**

PREP: **30 MINUTES**

COOK: **1 HOUR**

4 tbsp ghee

1 onion, finely chopped

3 bay leaves

4 green cardamom pods, bashed

2 black cardamom pods, bashed

1 star anise

1 cinnamon stick

1 tbsp cumin seeds

2 cloves

4 garlic cloves, grated

2.5cm piece fresh root ginger, peeled and grated

2 green chillies, chopped

1 tsp turmeric

1 tsp chilli powder

2 tsp garam masala

2 tbsp methi

1 baking potato, diced

200g cauliflower florets

150g green beans, cut into thirds

'SAL-T'. What a legend, we had to commemorate the boss Grandpa. I've been watching him feed young Asian kids for years, which has not only made me appreciate how much food we have access to in the UK, but also inspired me to try and help others as much as he did.

In a large saucepan, heat 2 tablespoons of the ghee and fry the onion for 15 minutes over a medium heat until caramelised. Add the bay leaves, cardamom, star anise, cinnamon stick, cumin seeds and cloves and fry for 2–3 minutes until toasty and fragrant, before adding the garlic, ginger, chillies, turmeric, chilli powder, garam masala and 1 tablespoon of the methi.

Fry for 5 minutes before adding all the vegetables and cashews.

Once all of the vegetables and cashews are in and well combined with the curry base, add the salt and 130ml water, cover and simmer for 15 minutes. The stir in the yoghurt and remove from the heat.

Meanwhile in a large pan of well-salted boiling water, cook the soaked rice for 7 minutes. Drain the rice and rinse briefly in cold water. Return to the pan, mix the remaining ghee and methi into the rice and check the seasoning.

Ingredients and method continued overleaf →

GRANDPA KITCHEN'S VEGETABLE BIRYANI

CONTINUED

1 large carrot, peeled and chopped

1 green pepper, diced

250g tomatoes, diced

150g frozen peas

100g cashews

1 tsp salt

100ml natural yoghurt

500g basmati rice, rinsed and soaked for 30 minutes

large handful of mint, roughly chopped

large handful of of fresh coriander, roughly chopped

Remove two-thirds of the curry from the pan and set aside in a bowl. Start to layer the biryani. Add a third of the rice on top of the curry, sprinkle over some of the herbs, then add half the curry set aside in the bowl. Add another layer of rice and herbs, then the remaining curry and then the remaining rice.

Cover the pot with a clean tea towel and a lid and put back over a low heat for 15 minutes to steam, then remove from the heat and leave to stand for 10 minutes untouched before serving.

V-GANG

Swap the ghee for oil and use coconut yoghurt to make this vegan.

ZA'ATAR & CHEESE MANAKEESH

(LEBANESE PIZZA)

MAKES: **6**

PREP: **20 MINUTES**

PROVE: **2 HOURS**

COOK: **15 MINUTES**

FOR THE DOUGH:

450g bread flour

1 tsp salt

210ml warm water

1 tbsp sugar

3 tbsp olive oil

7g sachet fast-action yeast

FOR ZA'ATAR MANAKEESH:

6 tbsp za'atar

6 tbsp olive oil, plus extra for drizzling

½ tsp salt

FOR CHEESE MANAKEESH:

100g grated mozzarella

30g halloumi cheese, grated

A Lebanese tradition – my mum used to send me to the shop to buy this for the family every weekend. The Italians thought that they ran the pizza game, little did they know my other brothers have been building it like the Burj Khalifa.

To make the dough, mix the flour and salt together in a large bowl or stand mixer. Combine the water, sugar, oil and yeast together in a jug and mix well. Leave to stand for 5 minutes until cloudy and fizzy. Make a well in the flour and pour in the wet ingredients.

If you are using a mixer, mix the dough slowly with a dough hook to start and then on a medium speed for 5 minutes until smooth and elastic. If you are making the dough by hand, stir the wet and dry ingredients together to mix, then use your hands to bring the dough together and transfer to a clean surface. Knead well for 5–8 minutes until smooth and elastic.

Place the dough in a clean, oiled bowl, cover with clingfilm and leave to prove in a warm place for 2 hours.

Preheat the oven to 230°C/210°C fan/Gas 8.

Divide the proved dough into 6 pieces, then roll into 15cm discs. Place the discs on baking sheets lined with baking parchment.

For the za'atar manakeesh, mix the za'atar and oil together with a pinch of salt and spread over 3 of the discs. Mix the grated mozzarella and halloumi together and sprinkle over the remaining 3 discs. You can also do a mix of cheese and za'atar on each disc, if you like.

Bake for 12–15 minutes until bubbling and golden, then drizzle with more olive oil while still hot.

HUMMUS & FALAFEL FOR LIFE

FOR THE HUMMUS:

250g dried chickpeas, soaked overnight (500g soaked weight)

1 tsp bicarbonate of soda

juice of 1 lemon

1 large garlic clove

2 tbsp tahini

1 tsp salt

2 small ice cubes

good-quality olive oil, to drizzle

sumac, to sprinkle

There's not a day that goes by without Tubsey mentioning falafel or hummus, so we had to put them in the book. I am Lebanese, so I may also have hummus in my veins. A great side dish, also vegan, you can't go wrong.

To make the hummus, having soaked the chickpeas overnight, transfer them to a large saucepan and cover with cold water. Mix in the bicarbonate of soda and bring to the boil, skimming any scum or skins that float to the top.

Simmer for about 1½ hours, skimming constantly, until the chickpeas are just tender enough to be crushed between your fingers. Drain the chickpeas, saving the cooking water, and pick away as many of the chickpea skins as possible – at least half is best for a silky hummus. Leave to cool completely.

When cooled, transfer to a food processor. Add the lemon juice, garlic, tahini, salt and 60ml of the reserved cooking water plus the ice cubes. Blend together until smooth and moussey. Serve immediately with the olive oil drizzled over and the sumac sprinkled over, alongside the falafel.

Adding the ice to your hummus will make it super-smooth and light.

FOR THE FALAFEL:

1.5l vegetable oil, for deep-frying (if using a saucepan; if using a deep-fat fryer follow manufacturer's instructions for oil)

225g dried chickpeas, soaked overnight (450g soaked weight)

1 small onion, quartered

20g coriander

10g parsley

4 garlic cloves

1 tsp salt

2 tsp ground cumin

2 tsp ground coriander

1 tsp ground cardamom

1 tbsp gram flour or plain flour

1 tsp baking soda

2 tbsp sesame seeds

To make the falafel, preheat the oil in a deep-fat fryer to 170°C or heat the oil in a deep saucepan over a medium-high heat to 170°C.

Drain the soaked chickpeas and dry off as much as possible before transferring to a food processor with the onion, herbs, garlic, salt, spices, flour and baking soda. Pulse together until you have a crumbly green mixture and everything is chopped relatively small.

Use an ice-cream scoop or spoon to shape the mixture into 12-14 falafels. The mixture will feel crumbly but use your hands to press it together. Sprinkle the falafel with the sesame seeds, then fry in batches until golden brown and crisp – they need to be fried soon after being mixed and shaped. Drain on kitchen paper and serve immediately.

SAAG PANEER BHAJI BUN

SERVES: **2**

PREP: **30 MINUTES**

COOK: **20 MINUTES**

2 brioche buns, halved

2 slices paneer or halloumi

FOR THE CORIANDER CHUTNEY:

60g coriander

20g sprigs of mint, leaves only

½ tsp ground cumin

2.5cm piece fresh root ginger, peeled and grated

juice of 1 lime

1 tsp caster sugar

30ml vegetable oil

FOR THE BHAJIS:

1.5l vegetable oil, for deep-frying (if using a saucepan; if using a deep-fat fryer follow manufacturer's instructions for oil), plus 2 tbsp vegetable oil for frying the cheese

45g gram flour

1 tsp ground cumin

1 tsp cumin seeds

½ tsp ground coriander

½ tsp hot chilli powder

¼ tsp salt

1 onion, finely sliced

FOR THE SAAG:

50g ghee

2 garlic cloves, grated

2.5cm piece fresh root ginger, peeled and grated

1 green chilli, sliced

1 tsp garam masala

1 tsp nigella seeds

200g baby spinach

Imagine a curry in a burger. Yeah, sounds messy, but hear me out. We put all the elements into beautiful compartments and presented it in a brioche bun. One of my favourite Indian dishes, that has been westernised, but the respect is still there.

Start by making the chutney. Place all the ingredients in a blender and blitz until smooth. Set aside. (This will make more chutney than you need, but it is great on grilled meat, fish or in cheese toasties.)

Preheat the oven to 180°C/160°C fan/Gas 4. Preheat the oil in a deep-fat fryer to 180°C or heat the oil in a deep saucepan over a medium-high heat to 180°C.

In a large bowl, whisk together the gram flour, spices and salt, then slowly whisk 60ml water until the mixture is similar in thickness to double cream. Mix in the onion and leave to sit for 5 minutes. This will make 4–6 bhajis.

When ready to fry, use 2 spoons to transfer bundles of the mixture to the hot oil carefully. After 1 minute, turn the bhajis in the oil and keep turning until they are evenly golden brown, then transfer to a baking sheet lined with kitchen paper. Keep warm in the oven while you toast the buns, fry the cheese and make the buttery saag.

Preheat the grill to hot and toast the brioche bun halves.

Heat 2 tablespoons of vegetable oil in a non-stick frying pan over a medium heat and gently fry the paneer or halloumi slices until golden brown and tender on both sides.

In another pan, heat the ghee over a medium heat until sizzling, then add the garlic, ginger, chilli and spices and fry for 2 minutes before adding the spinach. Wilt for 2–3 minutes in the spicy butter, then get ready to assemble.

First spread some chutney on the bottom half of a toasted bun, then top with a slice of cheese. Spoon on half the spinach, then top with 1 or 2 bhajis if you back yourself. Drizzle with more chutney and sandwich with the top half of the bun. Repeat to make the second bun. Serve with a cold beer.

SPANISH TORTILLA

SERVES: **2**

PREP: **15 MINUTES**

COOK: **35 MINUTES**

300ml plus 4 tbsp olive oil

1 large onion, finely sliced

2 baking potatoes (about 350g), peeled, halved lengthways and finely sliced into crescents

4 eggs, beaten

salt

warm crusty bread, to serve

Created by my Spanish bae. Trust me, when you've got someone special to impress, whip this one up for breakfast and chat to me later.

In a frying pan, heat 2 tablespoons of the olive oil over a medium heat and add the sliced onion. Cook for 15 minutes, stirring often until golden and soft.

At the same time, in another frying pan, heat the 300ml olive oil over a low heat. Add the potatoes and fry very gently for about 15-20 minutes until the potatoes are soft and starting to go golden. Using a slotted spoon carefully remove the potatoes from the oil and set aside to cool slightly in a bowl, draining off any excess oil.

Add the cooked onions to the bowl, season well and stir together. Mix the beaten eggs in and leave to sit for 5 minutes.

In a small, non-stick frying pan that is about 4cm deep, heat the remaining 2 tablespoons of oil over a low heat. Add the egg mixture and leave to set for 3 minutes. When you can see the edges beginning to set, put a plate on top of the pan and carefully but confidently flip the tortilla. Return the pan to the heat and gently slide the tortilla back into the pan to set on the other side. Cook for another 1 minute or so, then flip again.

Return to the pan as before and cook for 1½ minutes, then flip and return to the pan for a further 1½ minutes, before finally serving with warm crusty bread.

ALI'S PUMPKIN FESENJOON

V-GANG

SERVES: **6**

PREP: **20 MINUTES**

COOK: **2 HOURS**

2 tbsp olive oil

1 large onion, finely sliced

300g walnuts

650g peeled pumpkin or butternut squash (about 900g unprepped pumpkin), cut into 5cm chunks

1 tsp turmeric

1 tbsp sugar

1 tbsp tomato paste

1 tsp salt

80ml pomegranate molasses

150ml pomegranate juice

cooked rice, to serve

2 tbsp pomegranate seeds, to garnish

An Iranian dish that uses walnuts in a whole new way. Please message me when you see somebody use walnuts in a stew and then replace the meat with pumpkin, I beg.

In a large casserole, heat the oil and fry the onion gently over a low heat for 15 minutes until golden brown.

In a food processor, pulse the walnuts until they are finely chopped, then add to the onion. Cook for about 15 minutes until the walnuts are toasting and changing colour, then add the pumpkin or butternut squash, turmeric, sugar, tomato paste and salt.

Cook for 2 minutes, then stir in the pomegranate molasses, pomegranate juice and 600ml water. Simmer gently for 1½ hours, stirring often to make sure the mixture doesn't catch and adding a splash of water if necessary. The sauce will turn a rich brown.

Serve with rice and the pomegranate seeds sprinkled on top.

GOBI CURRY

50ml vegetable oil

2 onions, chopped

4 garlic cloves, grated

2.5cm piece fresh root ginger, peeled and grated

3 green chillies, sliced

3 tbsp Bengali five spice or 1 tsp each cumin seeds, coriander seeds, fennel seeds, nigella seeds, fenugreek seeds

1 tbsp turmeric

½ tsp ground cardamom

4 plum tomatoes, about 340g, roughly chopped

2 x 400ml tins coconut milk

2 bay leaves

1 small cauliflower (about 600g), cut into small florets

400g tin chickpeas, drained and rinsed

100g frozen peas

salt and ground black pepper, to taste

TO SERVE:

cooked basmati rice

100g pomegranate seeds

50ml coconut cream

30g toasted coconut

large handful of coriander, roughly chopped

Inspired by JME's 'munching on a Gobi' line, this is a curry that embraces vegetables and flavour, providing an overall experience of happiness in the mouth. For the ultimate V-Gang vibes, serve it up with my Sweet 'n' Sour Carrots recipe (see page 158).

In a large saucepan heat the oil, then add the onions. Fry over a medium heat for at least 15 minutes until soft and golden brown. Add the garlic, ginger and chillies and cook for 3–4 minutes before adding the spices and mixing well.

Cook for 2 minutes, adding a splash of water if the mixture starts to stick. Add the tomatoes and cook for a further 2 minutes before stirring in the coconut milk and bay leaves. Then add the cauliflower and chickpeas, season well and bring up to a simmer. Cook gently for 25 minutes until the cauliflower is soft and the sauce has thickened. Add the frozen peas and simmer for a further 4 minutes.

Serve with basmati rice and topped with the pomegranate seeds, coconut cream, toasted coconut and coriander.

Always brown your onions for a more intense flavour in your curry! Take your time with them – they need your love.

SIDES & SAUCES

'If a man does not have the sauce, then he is lost. But the same man can be lost in the sauce.' – Gucci Mane

THE BIG BANG BROCCOLI

SERVES: **2**

PREP: **10 MINUTES**

COOK: **10 MINUTES**

1.5l vegetable oil, for deep-frying (if using a saucepan; if using a deep-fat fryer follow manufacturer's instructions for oil)

2 large eggs, beaten

½ tsp Chinese five spice

60g cornflour

100g broccoli or tenderstem florets

60g panko breadcrumbs

flaky sea salt

FOR THE DIPPING SAUCE:

100g mayonnaise

1 tbsp hoisin sauce

1 tsp crispy chilli oil

1 tbsp sriracha

TO GARNISH:

2 spring onions, sliced

1 red chilli, sliced

You know anything that's called 'Big Bang' is going to be peng. I love broccoli, but when it's deep-fried and covered in sauce with extra sprinkles around the side, I sometimes feel myself becoming the broccoli. Love you brocc.

Preheat the oil in a deep-fat fryer to 180°C or heat the oil in a deep saucepan over a medium-high heat to 180°C.

Mix all the dipping sauce ingredients together in a bowl and set aside.

Beat the eggs, five spice and two-thirds of the cornflour together to form a smooth batter. Season with a pinch of salt.

When the oil is hot, working in batches, first toss the broccoli in the remaining cornflour, then coat in the batter and then toss in the breadcrumbs to lightly coat. Carefully place in the oil. Fry for 1 minute, turning if necessary, until the breadcrumbs are golden. Remove from the oil and drain on kitchen paper.

Season with flaky sea salt, garnish with the spring onions and chilli and serve with the dipping sauce.

Use cornflour instead of flour for a crispier, crunchier batter.

RAINBOW SALAD

V-GANG

¼ red cabbage, finely sliced

1 carrot, peeled and finely sliced

1 yellow pepper, finely sliced

1 Little Gem lettuces, finely sliced

1 courgette, shaved

3 spring onions, finely sliced

1 red chilli, finely sliced

handful of coriander leaves

handful of mint leaves

50g peanuts

FOR THE SATAY DRESSING:

75g smooth peanut butter

1 tbsp soy sauce

1 tbsp maple syrup

zest and juice of 1 lime

2.5cm piece fresh root ginger, peeled and grated

They say the eyes eat before the belly so this colourful salad makes sure you are ready. Good vibes, healthy life, it doesn't get better than this for your insides.

Divide all the vegetables between serving bowls, top with the coriander and mint leaves and sprinkle with the peanuts.

Whisk all the dressing ingredients together with 75ml water, adding more water if necessary to get a creamy thick dressing.

Dress the salad and serve. Add poached chicken, prawns or tofu if you need a protein hit.

HALLOUMI HAPPINESS FRIES

SERVES: **4 AS A SIDE**

PREP: **15 MINUTES**

COOK: **10 MINUTES**

2 x 250g block halloumi cheese

1l vegetable oil, for deep-frying (if using a saucepan; if using a deep-fat fryer follow manufacturer's instructions for oil)

30g plain flour

20g cornflour

1 tbsp ground coriander

FOR THE HARISSA YOGHURT:

150ml natural yoghurt

1 garlic clove, grated

2 tsp rose harissa paste

1 tsp tahini

salt and ground black pepper, to taste

TO SERVE:

2 tbsp dukkah

1 tsp black sesame seeds

handful of mint leaves

50g pomegranate seeds

Deep-fried cheese shaped like chips? That is a fat man dream with the extra tings on the side. The perfect accompaniment to any meal, no exceptions.

Cut the blocks of halloumi into chip-sized pieces and drain well on kitchen paper. Preheat the oil in a deep-fat fryer to 180°C or heat the oil in a deep saucepan over a medium-high heat to 180°C.

Mix the flour, cornflour and ground coriander together in a bowl and set aside.

Mix the yoghurt, garlic, harissa and tahini together in a bowl, season and set aside.

Toss the halloumi pieces in the flour mixture, dusting off any excess, before carefully placing in the hot oil. Do this in two or three batches if necessary. Fry the chips until they are a light golden brown all over, then carefully remove from the oil and drain on kitchen paper.

Sprinkle the dukkah and sesame seeds on the chips, then plate up along with the yoghurt, and garnish with the mint and pomegranate seeds.

MAC 'N' CHEESE BY THE ROUX LORD

SERVES: **4**

PREP: **15 MINUTES**

COOK: **40 MINUTES**

1l whole milk

50g butter

50g plain flour

1 tsp Dijon mustard

80ml double cream

120g Red Leicester, grated

100g Cheddar, grated

30g Parmesan, finely grated

100g grated mozzarella

fresh nutmeg

250g macaroni

salt and ground black pepper, to taste

FOR THE FILLINGS (OPTIONAL):

200g cooked lobster meat

1 leek and 200g spinach, wilted in butter

150g chargrilled red peppers, sliced

FOR THE TOPPINGS (OPTIONAL):

30g Flamin' Hot Cheetos, crushed

30g Toasted Chilli Panko (see page 158)

30g truffle-flavour crisps, crushed

Time and time again I have proven that I am The Roux Lord. But finally I'm writing down my powerful recipe for creating mac 'n' cheese. I have put years and years into developing this, and now it's yours, along with this book.

Heat the milk in a saucepan over a low-medium heat until just steaming. At the same time melt the butter in a large saucepan over a medium heat.

Whisk the flour into the butter to make a smooth roux and cook for about 1 minute. Then gradually add ladles of the hot milk into the roux, whisking well with each addition so the mixture is smooth, before adding more milk. When all the milk has been added, simmer for 5 minutes over a low heat to finish cooking out the flour.

Take off the heat and mix in the mustard, double cream, Red Leicester, Cheddar, Parmesan and half the mozzarella. Grate in some fresh nutmeg and season to taste. Keep the sauce warm over a gentle heat.

Preheat the grill to high or oven to 240°C/220°C fan/Gas 9.

Bring a large pan of well-salted water to the boil and add the macaroni. Cook for 7 minutes, then drain. Immediately mix the hot pasta into the cheese sauce, add any fillings, if using, then tip into a baking dish.

Top with the remaining mozzarella and any other additional toppings you might like!

If using a grill, pop the mac 'n' cheese under for 8-10 minutes until bubbling and golden. If using the oven, cook for 10-12 minutes until bubbling and golden on top. Serve immediately!

 Mix the hot pasta with the hot sauce, then simply brown the top for the sauciest creamy mac 'n' cheese. If the mixture gets cold it will dry out.

PERI-PERI CROQUETTES

SERVES: **4–6**

PREP: **25 MINUTES**

COOK: **1 HOUR 10 MINUTES**

3 medium baking potatoes

50g Cheddar, grated

100g grated mozzarella

2 tbsp peri-peri spice mix, or 1 tsp paprika and ½ tsp each garlic powder, onion powder and dried oregano

2 tsp chilli flakes

3 eggs

1 tsp salt

100g flour

100g panko breadcrumbs

2 eggs, beaten

1.5l vegetable oil, for deep-frying (if using a saucepan; if using a deep-fat fryer follow manufacturer's instructions for oil)

I used to only have croquettes at Christmas, but once I mixed it up and put all the extra love inside the mash, I'm trying to have it all the time.

Preheat the oven to 200°C/180°C fan/Gas 6. Bake the potatoes for 1 hour before scooping out the soft, cooked centre and mashing while still hot. Leave to cool completely.

Mix the mashed potato, cheeses, peri-peri, chilli flakes, 1 egg and the salt until smooth. Shape the mixture into 16 barrel-shaped croquettes.

Beat the remaining eggs in a bowl. Roll the croquettes in the flour, then egg, then coat in the panko and transfer to a baking sheet lined with baking parchment.

Chill in the fridge while you preheat the oil in a deep-fat fryer to 180°C or heat the oil in a deep saucepan over a medium-high heat to 180°C.

Fry the croquettes until golden brown and molten in the middle. Serve immediately.

RICE 'N' PEAS

V-GANG

200g dried red kidney beans, soaked overnight

1 onion, finely chopped

4 spring onions, finely chopped

2 garlic cloves, chopped

1 tsp allspice

1 tsp salt

1 tbsp All Purpose Seasoning

1 tbsp dried thyme

1 Scotch bonnet chilli, pierced

2.5cm piece fresh root ginger, peeled and grated

400ml tin coconut milk

400g basmati rice, rinsed

You don't have to be Jamaican to appreciate how good rice and peas are. And we're not talking plain basmati rice and garden peas right now, but a dish filled with love and depth. Here we're giving you the keys to Flavour Town.

Drain the beans and pop them into a large saucepan. Add the onion, spring onions, garlic, allspice, salt, All Purpose Seasoning, thyme, Scotch bonnet, ginger and coconut milk and cover with 1 litre of water.

Bring to the boil and simmer, covered, over a low-medium heat for 40 minutes until the beans are just tender. Add the rinsed rice and stir well, then cover again and cook gently over a low heat for 30 minutes, stirring every so often. Serve with the Jerk Chicken (see page 72).

ZUU HACKS

Pierce your Scotches for gentle heat; chop for a fierce heat.

THE FAT MO SALAD

V-GANG

SERVES: **2**

PREP: **15 MINUTES**

COOK: **25 MINUTES**

1 large aubergine (about 300g), sliced into 0.5cm rounds

75ml extra-virgin olive oil

1 red chilli, finely chopped

100g cherry tomatoes, roughly diced

juice of ½ lemon

1 garlic clove, crushed

handful of parsley, roughly chopped

handful of mint, roughly chopped

sea salt and ground black pepper, to taste

ZUU HACKS

Don't oil the aubergine before grilling – it will smoke you out of your kitchen.

If you didn't know already, I am the self-proclaimed Fat Mo Salah, due to my incredible football skills and my uncanny resemblance to Liverpool's legendary Egyptian forward and all-time top goal scorer in one Premier League season, Mohamed Salah. So obviously getting this pun into the book and sharing this wonderful aubergine salad was a double win for me.

Place a griddle pan over a high heat.

Working in batches, place the aubergine slices on the hot griddle and cook for 2 minutes, or until the underside has nicely charred. Turn the slices over and cook for a further 2 minutes. Set the grilled slices aside in a bowl.

When all the aubergine slices have been grilled, toss them in 2 tablespoons of the olive oil and a sprinkle of sea salt and set aside while you make the dressing.

To make the dressing, mix together the chilli, tomatoes, lemon juice, garlic and herbs with the remaining olive oil. Season well with salt and pepper. Lay the grilled aubergine slices on a serving plate and drizzle with the garlicky dressing. Serve immediately.

SWEET 'N' SOUR CARROTS

V-GANG

SERVES: **4**

PREP: **15 MINUTES**

COOK: **25 MINUTES**

700g carrots, peeled, halved lengthways and sliced on the diagonal

1 tsp salt

1 tbsp vegetable oil

3 garlic cloves, sliced

2 red chillies, sliced

4 spring onions, sliced

75ml soy sauce

75ml maple syrup

3 tbsp malt vinegar

handful of coriander leaves, roughly chopped, to serve

FOR THE TOASTED CHILLI PANKO:

25ml vegetable oil

1 tsp chilli flakes

60g panko breadcrumbs

½ tsp garlic powder

When I made this, people started going crazy, like they'd never had a carrot properly seasoned. Now I share with you a great way to enjoy a root vegetable that is often overlooked.

To make the toasted chilli panko, heat the oil in a frying pan over a medium heat. Add the chilli flakes and leave to infuse for 30 seconds before adding the panko and garlic powder. Stir the oil into the panko and keep moving around the pan gently, allowing the panko to toast to a lovely, even gold colour – 6-8 minutes.

Drain on some kitchen paper and set aside. This will keep for up to 1 week in an airtight container at room temperature.

To cook the carrots, cover with cold water in a saucepan, season with the salt and bring up to a simmer. Simmer for 5-8 minutes until just slightly tender, drain, cool slightly, then pat dry.

In a wok or large frying pan over a high heat, add the oil and then fry the carrots for about 2 minutes, allowing them to sit and caramelise on one side before turning and cooking the other side for a further 2 minutes. Add the garlic, chillies and spring onions and stir-fry for 1 minute before adding the soy, maple syrup and malt vinegar. Mix well and bring to a boil, allowing the liquid to reduce and become thick and glossy.

Serve topped with the toasted chilli panko and the coriander.

ZUU HACKS

Crispy panko is the way to go for extra crunch on salads, soups and pasta. Use different spices and flavourings to change it up.

FIRE RICE

V-GANG

2 tbsp olive oil

1 onion, chopped

1 red pepper, chopped

2 garlic cloves, grated

1 tsp hot smoked paprika

1 tsp ground cumin

1 tsp dried oregano

1 tsp chilli flakes

½ tsp turmeric

1 tbsp tomato paste

½ tsp salt

400g basmati rice, washed until the water runs clear

700ml Maggi, chicken or vegetable stock

Man loves rice and man loves spice, so instead of just boiling up some dead rice, take my word for it, this recipe tastes real nice.

In a large saucepan, heat the oil and fry the onion and pepper over a high heat for 10 minutes until they are softened and beginning to brown. Add the garlic and spices and cook for 2 minutes before stirring in the tomato paste and salt. Fry for 2 more minutes before gently stirring in the rice and stock.

Bring up to the boil, cover with a lid, turn the heat to medium and simmer for 12 minutes.

Then, without removing the lid, turn off the heat and leave to stand for 15 minutes. When ready to serve, remove the lid and fluff the rice with a fork.

JALAPEÑO COLESLAW

SERVES: **4**

PREP: **15 MINUTES**

200g (roughly ¼) white cabbage, finely shredded

150g (roughly ¼) red cabbage, finely shredded

1 large carrot, peeled and grated

50ml liquid from a jar of pickled jalapeños

4 spring onions, thinly sliced

2 tbsp chopped pickled jalapeños

50g soured cream

50g mayonnaise

handful of coriander leaves, roughly chopped (optional)

1 green jalapeño, chopped (optional)

salt and ground black pepper, to taste

Coleslaw can be so dead, but I want to give an honourable mention to the cole. A little bit of jalapeño in the mix goes a long way and gives this loyal sidekick the respect it deserves.

Mix the shredded cabbages and carrot together in a bowl. Pour over the pickle liquid and mix well. Leave to stand for 5 minutes before adding the rest of the ingredients and mixing well. Serve immediately.

MUMMA ZUU'S LENTILS

V-GANG

SERVES: **4 AS A SIDE OR 2 AS A MAIN**

PREP: **20 MINUTES**

COOK: **55 MINUTES**

2 tbsp vegetable oil

1 large onion, finely chopped

1 tsp turmeric

2 garlic cloves

2.5cm piece fresh root ginger, peeled

1 tsp salt

½ tsp chilli powder

1 tsp paprika

2 tsp ground cumin

2 tsp ground coriander

3 tomatoes, roughly chopped

1 red chilli, sliced

250g dried red lentils, washed

pinch each of black and white pepper

large handful of coriander, chopped, to serve

I used to hate this healthy ting growing up, but now I'm 25 I do appreciate a little bit of health. This dish is a great way to eat well, and also enjoy some of Mumma Zuu's magic flavours. You can't go wrong with a bit of a lentil.

In a large saucepan, heat the oil and fry half the onion over a medium heat for about 12 minutes until golden, adding the turmeric halfway through.

Meanwhile place the remaining onion, garlic, ginger and remaining spices in a food processor and blend to make a paste.

Add the paste to the frying onion and cook for 10 minutes before adding the chopped tomatoes and red chilli. Cook for 2 more minutes, then add the lentils, 1.2 litres of water and the pepper. Bring to a simmer and cook for about 30 minutes, until the lentils are tender and soft. Serve with the chopped coriander.

FATTOUSH SALAD

V-GANG

2 large Lebanese flatbreads

3 tbsp olive oil

4 plum tomatoes, quartered

½ cucumber, sliced

1 romaine lettuce, roughly chopped

3 spring onions, sliced

100g radishes, quartered

50g watercress

2 tsp sumac

large handful of mint, roughly chopped

handful of parsley, roughly chopped

sea salt

FOR THE DRESSING:

2 tbsp lemon juice

3 tbsp olive oil

2 tsp pomegranate molasses

salt and ground black pepper, to taste

This palate cleanser, which uplifts any dish with its crisp, crystal-clear flavour, was made by my Akhis. Fattoush is remixed across the world, but we are giving you a new version full of insight and love.

Preheat the oven to 200°C/180°C fan/Gas 6. Tear the flatbreads into rough 2cm pieces and toss in the olive oil and some sea salt. Lay out on a couple of baking sheets and bake for 15 minutes until crispy and golden, turning a couple of times while cooking.

To make the dressing, whisk together the lemon juice, olive oil, pomegranate molasses and salt and pepper.

Toss all the salad ingredients and bread together with the dressing and serve immediately.

This is a great way to use up stale flatbreads.

GETTIN' CHIPPY WIT IT

SERVES: **2**

PREP: **20 MINUTES**

COOK: **30 MINUTES**

1kg Maris Piper potatoes, peeled and cut into your preferred chip size

1 tbsp salt

1.5l vegetable oil, for deep-frying (if using a saucepan; if using a deep-fat fryer follow manufacturer's instructions for oil)

1 tsp Old Bay-style seasoning

½ tsp chilli powder

½ tsp garlic powder

dips, to serve

V-GANG

I love chips, but when they're soggy and dead it makes me want to cry. To make sure this never happens again, triple cook them and you're set for life. When man says season them, I mean don't stop until you've shown every chip the respect it deserves.

Add the potatoes to a pan and cover with cold water. Add the salt and bring to the boil. Simmer the potatoes for 10 minutes before carefully removing from the water and draining on kitchen paper. Leave to cool completely.

Preheat the oil in a deep-fat fryer to 140°C or heat the oil in a deep saucepan over a low heat to 140°C. Fry the chips in batches for about 3 minutes until they are just starting to crisp. Remove the chips from the pan and drain on kitchen paper immediately.

Mix together the Old Bay-style seasoning, chilli powder and garlic powder.

Crank the oil in the deep-fat fryer or saucepan up to 190°C. Cook the chips for a third time in batches until golden and super-crisp. Drain on kitchen paper, then toss in the seasoning. Serve with your favourite dips.

SCOTCH BONNET SAUCE

V-GANG

SERVES: **4**

PREP: **15 MINUTES**

COOK: **45 MINUTES**

2 tbsp vegetable oil

1 onion, finely chopped

1-2 Scotch bonnet chillies, depending on how hot you like it, pricked

4 garlic cloves, crushed

2.5cm piece fresh root ginger, peeled and grated

800g tomatoes, chopped

1 tbsp white vinegar

1 tbsp caster sugar

2 Maggi or other vegetable stock cubes

salt and ground black pepper, to taste

Don't be afraid of Scotch bonnet peppers – their sweetness makes for such an amazing flavour. After making this once you'll want to bang it on everything. The level of spice is definitely something everyone should be able to handle, it's all in the mind (and the capsaicin).

Add the oil to a saucepan and fry the onion over a medium heat for 15 minutes until soft and beginning to caramelise. Add the chillies, garlic and ginger and fry for 2-3 minutes more before adding the tomatoes, 3 tablespoons water, the vinegar, sugar and the stock cubes. Season with salt and pepper.

Bring up to a simmer and cook for 25 minutes to a thick, spicy sauce. Blend to a smooth sauce using a food processor or stick blender. Serve hot with meat, fish, vegetables, chips or with Jollof Rice Balls (see page 18).

GARLIC AÏOLI

V-GANG

SERVES: **2**

PREP: **15 MINUTES**

COOK: **40 MINUTES**

1 garlic bulb

olive oil, for drizzling

2 tsp white miso paste

1 tsp Dijon mustard

200ml soy milk

2 tbsp lemon juice

200ml vegetable oil

I used to think aïoli was a posh-man mayo. Now I realise it is definitely that, but you don't have to be posh to make it.

Preheat the oven to 200°C /180°C fan/Gas 6. Drizzle the garlic bulb with a bit of olive oil, then wrap in foil. Roast in the oven for 35-40 minutes until the garlic cloves are soft and tender. Leave to cool completely.

When cooled, squeeze the roast garlic flesh from the skins into a blender or food processor, then add the miso paste, mustard, soy milk and lemon juice. Blitz for 1 minute until smooth. Then slowly add the vegetable oil in a steady stream until fully incorporated and the aïoli is thick and creamy.

NACHO CHEESE SAUCINESS

410ml tin evaporated milk

120g Red Leicester, grated

120g Cheddar, grated

1 tbsp cornflour

1 red chilli, deseeded and finely chopped

1 tsp hot chilli powder

1 tbsp hot sauce

2 tbsps mayonnaise (optional, see Zuu hacks)

You can't go wrong with cheese sauce unless you can't eat cheese, but if you can eat cheese, then you might want to shower with this sauce.

Pour the evaporated milk into a saucepan and bring to a simmer over a medium heat. Mix the grated cheeses with the cornflour, then add to the pan along with chilli, chilli powder and hot sauce and whisk to combine. Simmer gently for 5 minutes until thickened, check the seasoning and, if using hot, serve immediately.

If you want to save your sauce to use as a cold dip later, stir in 2 tbsp of mayonnaise and leave to cool. This will stop it getting a skin!

Grate the cheese yourself rather than buying ready-grated cheese, as it contains preservatives that can make your sauce grainy.

BANGIN' BBQ SAUCE

SERVES: **2**

PREP: **5 MINUTES**

COOK: **15 MINUTES**

300g ketchup

60g dark brown sugar

1 tbsp malt vinegar

2 tsp smoked paprika

1 tsp Worcestershire sauce

1 tsp tomato paste

1 tsp soy sauce

50g honey

Forget ketchup, forget mayo, BBQ sauce is the flavour of love. It reminds me of my time in Texas, and it's just a great, sweet, punchy sauce that can go over anything. If you don't like barbecue we can't be friends.

Combine all the ingredients in a saucepan and bring up to a simmer over a low heat. Cook for 10–12 minutes until glossy and thickened.

SAUCE ALGÉRIENNE

SERVES: **4**

PREP: **10 MINUTES**

juice of ½ lemon

1 tsp ground cumin

1 tsp paprika

½ tsp chilli powder

1 tbsp tomato paste

1 tbsp harissa paste

1 small onion, finely chopped

240g mayonnaise

handful of coriander, finely chopped

salt and ground black pepper, to taste

Big up my ex on this one, this is a sick sauce used in Algeria and France for the bold harissa flavours. Try it on your wrap to take it to the next level.

Mix the lemon juice, cumin, paprika and chilli powder together in a bowl to form a paste. Add the tomato paste and harissa and stir to combine. Add the onion, mayonnaise, coriander and salt and pepper and whisk to combine.

SWEET POTATO MASH

SERVES: **4**

PREP: **10 MINUTES**

COOK: **30 MINUTES**

1kg sweet potato, peeled and roughly chopped

80g butter, diced

80ml double cream

fresh nutmeg

salt and ground black pepper, to taste

You know when you got your mash down, but you're trying to be a bit different? Enter the sweet potato, normal mash is dead. No, actually it's okay, but sweet potato is better.

Cover the sweet potato pieces in cold water, add 1 teaspoon salt and bring up to the boil. Simmer for 15–20 minutes until the sweet potato is super-tender. Drain and leave to dry out for 5 minutes.

Return the potato to the saucepan over a low heat. Use a masher to mash the potato or you can use a potato ricer. Add the butter and cream and mix well. Season with salt and pepper and a good grating of fresh nutmeg. Serve with the Unlimited Peri Chicken (see page 65).

FRIED PLANTAIN

SERVES: **4**

PREP: **10 MINUTES**

100ml vegetable oil

2 large, ripe plantains, sliced on the angle

salt

Ripe plantains are covered in dark brown spots – green plantains are not ripe!

Fried plantain or 'plantin' – doesn't matter how you say it, because eating it is going to bring you happiness. An African staple, a Caribbean love, also used in South American cuisine, this over-ripe banana is beautiful in all the ways, but we love it fried.

Heat the oil in a frying pan over a low-medium heat. The oil is hot enough when a slice of plantain gently sizzles.

Working in batches, gently lay in the plantain slices in the pan and leave to cook for 5–6 minutes, checking every couple of minutes. When they are golden brown, turn the slices over and repeat on the other side. When cooked the plantain should be golden, crisp and also tender in the middle. Drain on kitchen paper and serve sprinkled with salt.

This is seriously good served as a side to Granat Soup (see page 64).

DESSERTS

Who said we can't bake off?

AMSTERDAM CHURROS

MAKES: **12**

PREP: **20 MINUTES**

COOK: **20 MINUTES**

50g butter

250g plain flour

½ tsp salt

150g dark chocolate (50% cocoa solids), chopped

100ml double cream

50ml whole milk

25g golden syrup

50g caster sugar

1 tsp ground cinnamon

1.5l vegetable oil, for deep-frying (if using a saucepan; if using a deep-fat fryer follow manufacturer's instructions for oil)

Put oil on your scissors to help cut the batter.

When in Amsterdam, there often comes a time when we need to press the reset button. When this time comes there is only one thing that can bring back your taste buds and rejuvenate your mind, so we can do it all again. Step in the Amsterdam churro, smothered in oil and fake Nutella. It doesn't get better than this.

Heat the butter and 300ml water in a saucepan over a medium heat. Mix the flour with the salt. When the butter has completely melted and liquid has come to a boil, add in the flour mixture and beat well with a wooden spoon – just like making a roux.

Continue to beat until the mixture starts to come away from the sides of the pan. Remove from the heat and pop the mixture into a bowl. Cool for 10 minutes.

When the mixture has cooled slightly, transfer the batter to a piping bag fitted with a 2cm star nozzle in it. Cut out 6 pieces of baking parchment, each about 15 x 10cm. Then pipe 2 churros, each about 10cm long, onto each piece, using scissors to snip the end of the churro each time from the piping nozzle. Set aside while you make the chocolate sauce.

In a saucepan, gently heat together the chocolate, cream, milk and golden syrup over a low heat until you have a smooth and shiny sauce. Keep warm.

Mix the sugar and cinnamon together and place in a shallow bowl. Preheat the oil in a deep-fat fryer to 160°C or heat the oil in a deep saucepan over a low–medium heat to 160°C.

Lay the pieces of paper gently into the oil and when the churros release from each piece of paper, remove it. Fry the churros for 5–6 minutes until golden, then, using tongs, remove from the oil and place directly in the cinnamon sugar, tossing to coat.

Serve immediately with the hot chocolate sauce.

OLD SKL AUSSIE CRUNCH

150g margarine

75g caster sugar

25g golden syrup

120g self-raising flour, sifted

1½ tbsp cocoa powder, sifted

60g desiccated coconut

75g cornflakes, crushed

150g dark or milk chocolate, chopped

50g smooth peanut butter

Big up my Australian people, this is for you. To all my Aussie teachers who came over and taught me in primary school, this one's to show our appreciation for all things Australian and prove you're not just about kangaroos and spiders – you make desserts too.

Preheat the oven to 200°C/180°C fan/Gas 6. Grease and line a 20 x 20cm brownie tin with baking parchment.

Melt together the margarine, sugar and golden syrup in a saucepan over a medium heat, stirring until smooth. Then take off the heat and add the flour, cocoa powder, coconut and cornflakes and mix until well combined.

Spoon the mixture into the prepared tin and press in well so it forms an even layer and is well pressed into the corners. Bake for 15–20 minutes until just set, then remove from the oven and leave to cool completely in the tin.

When the crunch has cooled completely, melt the chocolate in a glass bowl over some just simmering water, or in the microwave in 20-second bursts. Then heat the peanut butter in the microwave for 45 seconds until it is hot and slightly more runny.

Spread the chocolate over the cooled crunch, taking care to get it in an even layer over the top. Using a teaspoon, dollop the peanut butter over the chocolate layer. Using a cocktail stick or chopstick, drag the pointy end through the peanut butter and chocolate to create swirls. Chill in the fridge for 1 hour to set the chocolate before cutting into 9 squares.

MINT CHOC-CHIP ICE CREAM CAKE

SERVES: **8**

PREP: **30 MINUTES**

FREEZE: **6½+ HOURS**

FOR THE CAKE:

250g mascarpone

180g condensed milk

2 tbsp green food colouring

400ml double cream

15ml peppermint extract

100g golden syrup

60g dark chocolate, chopped, or chocolate chips

FOR THE BASE:

50g butter

100g dark chocolate

40ml golden syrup

70g waffle cones (about 6 cones), crushed

40g chopped roasted hazelnuts

pinch of sea salt

TO DECORATE:

40g dark chocolate

20g chopped roasted hazelnuts

This is a mash-up of two classic bossman shop ice creams – Viennetta and Cornetto – that man has bought so many times, but never thought it could be made in his yard. This recipe is to prove we can all be our own version of Mr Whippy without any of his special machinery. And don't worry, if you're not on a mint vibe, you can change the flavour to suit all your frozen dreams.

Line a 900g loaf tin with clingfilm, leaving excess over the edges.

In a large bowl, whisk together the mascarpone, condensed milk and half the food colouring until smooth. In a separate bowl, whip the cream, peppermint extract, golden syrup and the remaining food colouring to soft peaks. Gently fold the mascarpone mixture into the whipped cream, followed by the chocolate.

Fill the loaf tin with the mixture, making sure to level off the top for a smooth surface. Place in the freezer for 6 hours minimum or overnight.

For the base, melt together the butter, dark chocolate and golden syrup in a saucepan over a very low heat. Take off the heat and mix in the crushed cones, hazelnuts and a pinch of salt.

Remove the cake from the freezer and press the chocolate mixture onto the surface of the cake, using a rolling pin to level out the top. Return to the freezer for 30 minutes.

To serve, melt the dark chocolate in a glass bowl over some just-simmering water, or in the microwave in 20-second bursts. Remove the cake from the freezer and leave for 10 minutes to warm slightly before turning out, chocolate-base-side down, onto a plate or board. Drizzle all over with the melted chocolate and sprinkle with the chopped hazelnuts.

THE WAFFLE BAGUETTE TOWER

SERVES: **2**

PREP: **15 MINUTES**

COOK: **20 MINUTES**

FOR THE FRENCH TOAST:

3 eggs

200ml whole milk

3 tbsp soft brown sugar

1 tsp vanilla extract

½ tsp ground cinnamon

6 slices baguette

25g butter

icing sugar, for dusting

FOR THE BERRY COMPOTE:

125g mixed frozen berries

25g caster sugar

zest and juice of ½ lemon

FOR THE WHITE CHOCOLATE SAUCE:

100g white chocolate, chopped

100ml double cream

Use any leftover bread to make French toast – the staler the better.

When Natasia Demetriou told me about her dad's obsession with baguettes and never throwing them away, but eventually flushing them down the toilet, we had to figure out a way to create a dessert out of them. So we covered them in a beautiful eggy batter, placed them on some cooked-down summer fruits and finished them off with a dusting of icing sugar. This is one of the greatest dishes I've ever had, and it's a good way to use up old bread.

Whisk the eggs, milk, brown sugar, vanilla and cinnamon together in a large dish, add the baguette slices and set aside to soak for 20 minutes.

Meanwhile, in a saucepan, mix the berries with the sugar and lemon juice and bring up to a simmer over a low heat. Cook gently for 8-10 minutes until you've got a lovely, shiny compote.

To make the white chocolate sauce, put the chocolate into a bowl. Heat the cream in saucepan over a low heat until it's just about to boil, then pour over the chocolate. Leave to stand for 1 minute before stirring. The chocolate will melt into the cream to form a smooth sauce.

Heat the butter in a large frying pan until just foaming over a low-medium heat. Lift the baguette slices out of the egg mixture and allow any excess to drip off before placing them in the foaming butter. Cook for 4-5 minutes, turning when golden brown and cook for a further 4-5 minutes.

Plate the pieces of hot French toast and dust with a bit of icing sugar, then drizzle the fruit compote and white chocolate sauce over the top for a super-indulgent dessert.

KEY LIME PIE POTS

45g digestive biscuits

45g speculoos biscuits

45g unsalted butter

160ml double cream

160g condensed milk

160g cream cheese

zest and juice of 4 limes

Brown the butter for the biscuit crumb for a delicious nuttiness.

I should be selling these in supermarkets with my face on the lid, but I'm passing on the recipe for the world to enjoy. When we made these for Jamali, there was a little hair in his pot. To this day, I believe he planted it there because he wants my spot on Dave.

To make the base, put both kinds of biscuit in a plastic food bag and crush to a fine crumb with a rolling pin or pulse both kinds of biscuit until crumbly in a food processor. Place in a bowl.

Heat the butter in a small saucepan over a medium heat. When it starts to foam and sizzle, keep watch until the butter has turned a golden brown and smells nutty. Remove from the heat and mix into the crushed biscuits.

Fill the bases of 4 jars or ramekins with 2cm of crumb each, saving a little for decoration, and chill in the fridge while you make the filling.

In a bowl, whisk together the cream, condensed milk, cream cheese, zest of 3 of the limes and juice of all 4 until smooth. Top the biscuit bases with this creamy mixture and return to the fridge to chill for 1 hour or so, or overnight. Before serving, sprinkle with the extra lime zest and the remaining nutty, buttery biscuit crumb.

CHERRY SPOTTED DICK JAM ROLY POLY

175g self-raising flour, plus extra to dust

50g caster sugar

100g vegetable suet

100g dried cherries

125g cherry jam

hot custard, to serve

More English than Harry Redknapp, made for Harry Redknapp. This dish is funny to say, but is so good to eat. A combination of two classic British staples and made by an ethnic refugee.

Fill and boil the kettle. Cut a piece of baking parchment into a 50 x 40cm rectangle, and cut a piece of foil to roughly the same size. Grease the piece of baking parchment with a little oil or butter and place it on top of the foil, greased-side up.

In a bowl, mix the flour, half the sugar and the suet together, gently rubbing in the suet until it forms a breadcrumb texture. Mix in the dried cherries. Using a knife, gradually stir in 90ml water until the mixture starts to come together, then use your hands to form a shaggy dough.

Preheat the oven to 180°C/160°C fan/Gas 4.

On a floured surface, roll the dough out to form a rectangle roughly 30 x 20cm. Spread the jam all over, leaving a 2cm border all the way around. Then tightly roll the long side away from you to form a 30cm log. Press the ends together to seal gently and place on the greased sheet of greaseproof paper with the seam at the bottom. Bring the paper and foil together loosely around the log, sealing well but leaving space for the roll to rise. Place onto a rack or small baking tray within a bigger oven tray. Fill the tray about one-third up with hot water. Place in the oven and bake for 1 hour 20 minutes.

Leave to stand for 10 minutes before unwrapping the parcel. Sprinkle the remaining sugar on top and roll the log in the sugar that falls onto the paper to coat it evenly in sugar. Slice and serve with hot custard.

SWEDISH CINNAMANDEM BUNS

MAKES: **6**

PREP: **15 MINUTES**

COOK: **20 MINUTES**

60g caster sugar

1 tbsp ground cinnamon

½ tsp ground cardamom

pinch of salt

350g roll ready-made chilled croissant dough

3 tbsp golden syrup

2 tbsp pearl sugar

ZUU HACKS

Ready-made croissant dough is your best friend. You can use it to top pies, deep-fry it for cronuts or fill it with cheese and tomato and never go to Pret again.

We needed to give Maya Jama the VIP treatment, so we knew a Swedish-inspired *fika* would take her back to her childhood in Sweden. Seeing these at the shops, I've always wondered how to make them. Can't lie, it's proppa long so we made a shortcut recipe that is just as good. Hang tight shop-bought pastry.

Preheat the oven to 200°C/180°C fan/Gas 6. Grease a 6-hole deep muffin tin lightly with vegetable oil.

Mix the caster sugar with the cinnamon, cardamom and salt in a bowl and set aside.

Unroll the croissant dough and remove the pieces on either end so you have 4 triangles in a rectangular sheet. (Use the leftover pieces of dough to make the Old Skl Cheese 'n' Tomato Pastries on page 38.)

Scatter the spiced sugar evenly over the sheet of dough, then roll up the short end to form a thick log. Trim the uneven edges off, then cut into 6 even pieces. Place the rolls carefully in the muffin tin and bake for 20 minutes until risen and golden.

Take the buns out of the oven and carefully remove them from the muffin tin while still hot to prevent sticking.

Heat the golden syrup in a pan over a gentle heat and brush over the buns to glaze them. Sprinkle with the pearl sugar and serve still warm.

AKARA
(AFRICAN DOUGHNUTS)

MAKES: **12**

PREP: **15 MINUTES**

STAND: **1 HOUR**

COOK: **20 MINUTES**

4 medium overripe bananas (about 350g), mashed

130g rice flour

1.5l vegetable oil for frying, (if using a saucepan; if using a deep-fat fryer follow manufacturer's instructions for oil), plus 1 tbsp vegetable oil

1 tsp baking powder

1 tsp grated nutmeg, plus extra for dusting

1 tsp tomato paste

pinch of salt

3 tbsp caster sugar, plus extra for dusting

An African dish that differs from place to place. I'm giving you a version of my mum's recipe. Please don't judge me or message me on Twitter banging on about how it's not the way it's done – everyone has a different recipe, so this is mine.

Combine the bananas with the rice flour, the 1 tablespoon vegetable oil, baking powder, nutmeg, tomato paste, salt, sugar and 80ml water to make a batter. Leave to stand for 1 hour.

Preheat the oil in a deep-fat fryer to 160°C or heat the oil in a deep saucepan over a low-medium heat to 160°C.

When ready to fry, use two spoons or an ice-cream scoop to dollop golfball-sized pieces of the batter in the hot oil. Fry the akara for 4–5 minutes until golden brown and crisp. Serve immediately, dusted in more sugar and nutmeg.

BANOFFEE PIE SURPRISE

SERVES: **8**

PREP: **30 MINUTES**

CHILL: **4+ HOURS**

262g packet chocolate digestive biscuits

80g butter, melted

397g tin ready-made caramel or 350g dulce de leche

2 (90g) crunchy chocolate bars (e.g. Lion, Snickers, Kit Kat), chopped into 1cm pieces

40g salted peanuts, chopped, plus extra to decorate

3 large ripe bananas

450g double cream

1 tbsp vanilla bean paste

½ tsp ground cinnamon

1 square (about 20g), dark chocolate, grated, to decorate (optional)

I will never forget when a man in Chinatown told us that little bananas are real bananas and big bananas are fake bananas. Don't get it twisted though, you can use whatever banana you like for this one. For the surprise element levels, add in your favourite crunchy chocolate bar. Have you ever mixed a Lion bar with caramel? Just know it tastes like caramel.

To make the base, put the biscuits in a plastic food bag and crush to a fine crumb using a rolling pin or pulse in a food processor until crumbly, then stir in the melted butter.

Grease a 22cm round tart tin. Pour in the biscuit mixture and press into the tin using the back of a spoon to form an even base, taking care to press into the fluted edges. Chill in the freezer for 20 minutes.

Pour the caramel or dulce de leche into the biscuit case then sprinkle with the chopped chocolate bars and peanuts. Chill in the fridge for 4–6 hours.

When ready to serve, slice the bananas on the diagonal and lay on top, completely covering the base. Whip the cream, vanilla and cinnamon together to soft peaks and dollop over the bananas in cloud-like pillows. Top with more chopped peanuts and grated dark chocolate, if you like.

NO LONG PEANUT BUTTER CUP 'N' PRETZEL ICE CREAM

SERVES: **6–8**

PREP: **25 MINUTES**

CHILL: **6 HOURS**

397g tin condensed milk

250g mascarpone

30g golden syrup

1 tbsp vanilla extract

50g cocoa powder, sifted

600ml double cream

150g peanut butter cups, roughly chopped, plus extra to decorate

100g smooth peanut butter

50g pretzels, crushed, plus extra to decorate

20g salted peanuts, roughly chopped

ADDITIONAL SERVING SUGGESTIONS (OPTIONAL):

mini peanut butter cups

mini candy-coated chocolate buttons

chocolate-covered pretzels

salted caramel sauce

Not everyone has an ice cream maker and not everyone likes ice cream. Well, guess what? This is going to change both of those things. No long, no churn.

In a large bowl, whisk together the condensed milk, mascarpone, golden syrup and vanilla until completely smooth. Divide this mixture between two bowls.

Into one bowl, stir in the cocoa powder until fully combined, then add half the cream. Whip to a soft peaks, stir in the peanut butter cups and set aside.

Whisk half the peanut butter into the other bowl until fully combined, then add the remaining cream and whisk to a soft peak. Stir in the pretzels and set aside.

Heat the remaining peanut butter in the microwave in 20-second bursts or over a gentle heat in a pan so that it is just runny enough to drizzle, and leave to cool slightly.

In a 900g loaf tin, add a few tablespoons of the chocolate ice cream, then dollop over some of the peanut ice cream, drizzle some peanut butter over and use the end of a spoon to lightly swirl. Continue to layer and swirl the ice creams and peanut butter, then cover and freeze for at least 6 hours before serving.

Remove from freezer and leave to stand for 20 minutes before serving topped with the chopped peanuts and more crushed pretzels and chopped peanut butter cups.

Condensed milk makes the ice cream super-smooth and soft.

PBJ CHEESECAKE

SERVES: **6–8**

PREP: **30 MINUTES**

CHILL: **4+ HOURS**

vegetable oil, for greasing

150g digestive biscuits

75g butter, melted

½ tsp salt

170g smooth peanut butter

225g cream cheese

100g caster sugar

2 tsp vanilla extract

225ml double cream

40g icing sugar, sifted

60g frozen raspberries

100g seedless raspberry jam

40g salted peanuts, crushed

I don't think it gets greater than taking classic snacks and combining them with other classic snacks. I've always wondered how far can we take PBJ. Well, my friend, we've taken it to the next level. That jam on the peanut butter cheesecake is basically mouth heaven.

Grease a 20cm springform tin with vegetable oil. To make the base, put the biscuits in a plastic food bag and crush to a fine crumb using a rolling pin or pulse in a food processor until crumbly, then stir in the melted butter and salt to make a sandy mixture.

Using a spoon, press this into the bottom of the tin to make a smooth, even base. Chill in the freezer while you make the filling.

Using a stand mixer or hand whisk, combine the peanut butter, cream cheese, caster sugar and vanilla until smooth and well mixed. In a separate bowl, lightly whip the cream and icing sugar together until very softly whipped, then fold into the cream cheese mixture and mix until well combined.

Spoon the filling into the tin and spread over the base to make a smooth, even layer. Chill for 4–6 hours in the fridge.

To make the jam drizzle, heat together the frozen raspberries and jam in a saucepan over a medium heat. Bring to the boil and cook for 5 minutes or so until thickened, then remove from the heat and cool completely in a bowl.

When you are ready to serve, remove the cheesecake from the tin, drizzle over the jam drizzle and sprinkle with the peanuts.

BAKLAVA

MAKES: **24**

PREP: **30 MINUTES**

COOK: **1 HOUR**

250g golden caster sugar

1 tbsp orange blossom extract

juice of ½ lemon

80g walnuts

80g pecans

250g packet filo pastry

100g ghee or clarified butter, melted

Swap any nuts you like into the mix.

Any good Turkish or Lebanese restaurant knows that, when the bill comes, it must be with a side of baklava. We are showing you how to make this so when the bill comes, you can actually say, 'Sorry, I make my own.'

Add 220g of the golden caster sugar, water, orange blossom extract and lemon juice to a saucepan with 100ml water and bring to a boil. Simmer over a medium heat for 5 minutes until slightly thickened, then remove from the heat and leave it to cool completely.

Preheat the oven to 160°C/140°C fan/Gas 5.

Blitz the walnuts and pecans with the remaining caster sugar in a food processor until they resemble breadcrumbs.

Trim all the sheets of filo pastry to the same size as a 32 x 22cm rectangular tin. Brush the bottom of the tin with ghee or clarified butter, then lay half of the filo sheets in the bottom. Cover with the nut mix, then lay the other half of the filo on top.

Brush the top sheet with ghee, then cut four deep lines through the sheets lengthways down the tin. Then cut six deep diagonal lines through the sheets across the tin to get the diamond-shaped baklava. Pour over the remaining ghee and bake for 1 hour until golden brown.

Remove from the oven and immediately pour over the cooled syrup. Leave to cool for 30 minutes before serving.

BIG DRIP CHOCOLATE CAKE

260g cocoa powder, sifted

110g dark chocolate, chopped

300g light brown sugar

½ tsp salt

30g unsalted butter, softened

230ml black coffee

4 large eggs

2 egg yolks

175g plain flour

2 tsp bicarbonate of soda

3 honeycomb chocolate bars, crushed

You may have seen these cakes on Instagram, you may have paid a baker incredible amounts of money to make one of these cakes. We here on *Big Eats* want to empower you to take the risk and make one yourself.

Grease and line two 20cm round cake tins. Preheat the oven to 200°C /180°C fan/Gas 6.

Put the cocoa powder, chocolate, sugar and salt in a large bowl. Put the butter and coffee into a saucepan and bring to a simmer over a low heat, then pour over the cocoa powder mixture and whisk together until the chocolate has melted and the mixture is smooth.

Beat the eggs and egg yolks together and whisk into the chocolate mixture, followed by the flour and bicarbonate of soda.

Divide the mixture between the prepared tins, then bake for 30-35 minutes until springy and a skewer inserted into the centre of the cakes comes out clean. Leave the cakes to cool in their tins for 20-30 minutes, then turn out onto wire racks and cool completely.

Meanwhile, to make the chocolate buttercream, melt the chocolate gently in a glass bowl over some just-simmering water, or in the microwave in 20-second bursts and leave to cool slightly.

Using a stand mixer or electric beaters, whip the butter for 4-5 minutes until pale and fluffy. Add half the icing sugar, stirring it in gently before whipping until fully combined. Add the remaining icing sugar and repeat the whipping process until you have a super-smooth and whipped buttercream. Fold in the melted chocolate until fully combined.

FOR THE CHOCOLATE BUTTERCREAM:

160g dark chocolate, chopped

250g unsalted butter, softened

450g icing sugar, sifted

FOR THE GANACHE:

70g double cream

70g dark chocolate (50% cocoa), chopped

Trim the tops of the cooled sponges to make them level. Spread 3 tablespoons of buttercream over one of the sponges, leaving a 1cm border all the way around. Sprinkle over half the crushed honeycomb chocolate, then top with the other sponge. Use the rest of the buttercream to cover the cake entirely, smoothing out the top so it is as level as possible.

To make the ganache, heat the cream over a low heat until it is just simmering, then pour over the chocolate. Leave to stand for 1-2 minutes, then stir until you get a smooth ganache. Check the thickness of the ganache - if it runs down the side of the bowl and stops, it is ready to use! If it is too runny leave to sit for another 1-2 minutes.

Put the ganache in a piping bag or squeezy bottle and carefully drizzle all around the edge of the cake. Then fill in the top with the rest of the ganache and crumble over the remaining honeycomb chocolate. Leave to set in the fridge for 30 minutes before serving.

Use dark chocolate with a lower percentage of cocoa for your ganache to achieve the perfect consistency.

SPRINKLE CAKE 'N' CUSTARD

400g plain flour, sifted

1 tbsp baking powder

1 tsp bicarbonate of soda

1 tsp salt

350g caster sugar

135ml vegetable oil

3 large eggs

1 tbsp vanilla extract

100g soured cream

380ml whole milk

hot custard, to serve

FOR THE ICING:

40g fresh raspberries or 40g frozen raspberries, defrosted

juice of 1 lemon

350g icing sugar, sifted

1–2 drops of pink food colouring

2 tbsp hundreds and thousands or rainbow sprinkles

Taking you back to primary school. Imagine the simple joy of hot custard melting the icing off the cake, creating a homogeneous liquid of sweetness and dreams. Forget boujie desserts, it doesn't get better than sprinkle cake and custard.

Grease and line a deep 34 x 24cm rectangular brownie tin. Preheat the oven to 200°C/180°C fan/Gas 6.

In a large bowl, combine the flour, baking powder, bicarbonate of soda, salt and sugar. In another bowl whisk together the oil, eggs, vanilla, soured cream and milk until well mixed. Add the wet mixture to the dry and whisk together with electric beaters until you have a smooth cake batter.

Pour into the prepared tin and bake in the middle of the oven for 50 minutes, until a skewer inserted into the centre of the cake comes out clean. Leave to cool completely in the tin.

When the cake is cooled, mix the raspberries and lemon juice together, crushing the raspberries to make a purée. Strain the purée through a fine sieve and discard the seeds. Add the purée to the icing sugar and stir gently to combine, adding a drop of food colouring and a splash of water, if needed, to make a thick but spreadable icing.

Turn the cake out onto a board or large plate and spread over the sticky pink icing. Sprinkle over the hundreds and thousands or rainbow sprinkles and slice into 12 squares. Serve with hot custard.

Cake batters that use oil and soured cream are super-moist! This cake keeps for up to a week in an air-tight container and it's huge, so you need a week to eat it.

Stir 150g chocolate chips tossed in 1 teaspoon of plain flour into the cake batter before cooking and use Chocolate Buttercream (see page 201) for an amazing choc-chip cake.

FRESH CRÊPES

MAKES: **8**

PREP: **10 MINUTES**

CHILL: **30 MINUTES**

COOK: **25 MINUTES**

150g plain flour, sifted

pinch of salt

1 tbsp caster sugar

3 eggs, beaten

300ml whole milk

25g butter, melted and cooled slightly

50g butter, for frying

SERVING SUGGESTIONS:

chocolate hazelnut spread

mixed berries

banana

lemon juice

icing sugar

whipped cream

Big up my ex Sabrina for teaching me about all the Frenchie tings. For me, there is nothing more French than a nice hot crêpe filled with jam, then another hot crêpe filled with chocolate hazelnut spread. Oui oui.

Sift the flour into a bowl and mix with the salt and sugar. Whisk together the eggs and milk. Make a well in the centre of the flour, then slowly whisk in the egg mixture, trying to avoid lumps - you can do this with electric beaters. When all the egg and milk is mixed in and the batter is smooth, transfer to a jug and rest in the fridge for 30 minutes. Remove the batter from the fridge and whisk in the melted butter.

Heat a frying pan over a medium heat and rub with a small amount of the butter for frying. When the butter is foaming, pour in a small amount of batter, about half a ladle, and swirl the pan around so that the batter coats the pan.

Cook for 2-3 minutes, then flip when the edges just start to go golden. Cook for 1 minute on the other side. Keep warm while you make the rest of the crêpes and serve with your toppings of choice!

Use a squeezy bottle for the pancake batter and write a message in pancake form.

HONEY NUT CHEERIO BARS

MAKES: **12**

PREP: **15 MINUTES**

COOK: **15 MINUTES**

CHILL: **2 HOURS**

120g Honey Nut Cheerios

150g flaked almonds

150g honey

80g coconut oil

½ tsp ground cinnamon

pinch of flaky sea salt

cold milk, for dunking
(optional)

This one here just proves that cereal is the greatest creation after juice. I do love juice. This is a very simple recipe that will provide you with all the energies and a nice treat to have at home.

Preheat the oven to 180°C/160°C fan/Gas 4. Grease and line a 20 x 20cm square tin.

Spread the Cheerios and almonds on two baking sheets and toast in the oven for 10-15 minutes until lightly golden and fragrant. Cool for 5 minutes before mixing together in a large bowl.

Heat the honey and coconut oil in a saucepan over a low heat, bringing up to a simmer. Stir in the cinnamon and salt, then pour over the Cheerios and almonds. Mix well, making sure the Cheerios and almonds are well coated. Spoon the mixture into the prepared tin and press down well. Leave to cool before chilling in the fridge for 2 hours.

Slice into 12 and serve with cold milk for dunking, if you like.

DRINKS

Liquid happiness

BIG ZUU'S BISSAP

25ml hibiscus syrup

25ml pomegranate juice

50ml ginger beer

25ml Courvoisier or other cognac

juice of 2 limes, plus lime wedges, to garnish

4–5 large ice cubes

pomegranate seeds, to garnish

This drink is a combination of my love for Courvoisier and Christmas waves. People normally don't know how to make a cocktail with brandy but, as a brandy connoisseur, I have trialled and errored many a time to find a perfect balance for such a drink. I present to you the Big Zuu Bissap.

Stir all the ingredients together in a large glass to combine, then serve garnished with lime slices and pomegranate seeds.

MANGO LASSI LEVELS

150g fresh mango (about
1 small mango), peeled,
stoned and roughly chopped

120g natural yoghurt

pinch of ground cardamom

2 ice cubes

1 tsp soft brown sugar

3 tbsp water

TO GARNISH (OPTIONAL):

chopped pistachios

saffron strands

When eating spicy food some people like to have yoghurt on the side, but my Asian brothers thought, 'You know what? That's a bit plain. Why don't we add some mango into the game?' Since then, this is the only lassi I need.

Blitz all the ingredients together in a blender or smoothie maker until smooth, thick and creamy. Pour into a glass and serve immediately with chopped pistachios and saffron strands on top, if you like.

OREO MILKSHAKE

8 Oreo biscuits

1 plant-based choc ice of your choice

3 scoops plant-based vanilla ice cream

½ tsp vanilla extract

130ml oat milk

2 tbsp plant-based chocolate sauce

vegan whipped cream, to top

When you are this black and this lactose intolerant, the thought of never eating dairy again fills you with pain and anguish. Then I discovered there are other versions of dairy that don't make you run to the toilet, so I present to you the vegan Oreo milkshake. Tinseltown, eat your heart out.

Place 6 of the Oreos in a blender with the choc ice, ice cream, vanilla extract and oat milk and blend. Drizzle the inside of a glass with some of the chocolate sauce, then pour in the milkshake. Top with vegan cream, the remaining chocolate sauce and the remaining 2 Oreos, crushed.

PICKLEBACKS

50ml whiskey

50ml liquid from a jar
of pickles

Now, I only did this to please a *Big Eats* customer a.k.a.
Rosie Jones. She somehow forced me to take a shot of pickle
juice accompanied by a shot of whiskey and convinced me
that it would taste like a cheeseburger. The only thing left
for you to do is try it yourself!

Serve one 25ml shot of whisky with one 25ml shot of pickle
liquid to chase.

PINEAPPLE POWER TEA

1 star anise

2.5cm piece fresh root
ginger, peeled and sliced

2cm piece fresh turmeric,
peeled and sliced (it will
stain your fingers so take
care)

1 cinnamon stick, broken

300g pineapple skin

1 tbsp caster sugar

juice of 1 lemon

To acquire the length and strength, you must take on
remedies from the tropical island of Jamaica. With all their
knowledge and teachings, we whittled it down into a formula
mixed with boiled pineapple juice, to provide you with the
elixir needed to get a whine in the rave.

Fill a small piece of muslin with the star anise, ginger, turmeric
and cinnamon and tie to secure. Heat 400ml water, the pineapple
skin, sugar and lemon juice in a saucepan with the spice bag and
bring to a simmer, then turn off the heat and infuse for 30 minutes.
Serve immediately.

ATAY

SERVES: **2**

PREP: **5 MINUTES**

(MOROCCAN MINT TEA)

2 green tea bags

4 large sprigs of mint, plus mint leaves, to garnish

1 tbsp caster sugar

Growing up in West London I had a lot of Moroccan friends. Going to their houses was always a great vibe. You would sit on their wonderful Moroccan sofa and be handed a small cup of beautiful mint tea. You can never go wrong with a tea, and even better if there's a little tagine on the side.

Add all the ingredients and 350ml water to a saucepan. Bring to the boil and simmer for 5 minutes. Serve garnished with mint leaves.

RUM PUNCH

SERVES: **2**

PREP: **5 MINUTES**

25ml spiced rum

25ml coconut rum

25ml pineapple juice

25ml grenadine syrup

25ml mango juice

25ml orange juice

juice of 2 limes, plus lime wedges, to garnish

25ml syrup from a tin of fruit cocktail, plus the fruit, to garnish

ice cubes

It's not a party if there's no rum punch. The classic white person will be put off by the sheer amount of sugar in such a drink, but we ethnics storm forward into the field of diabetes without looking back.

Combine all the ingredients together in a jug and pour into a glass over ice. Garnish with some of the fruit cocktail and lime wedges and serve.

GUINNESS* PUNCH

SERVES: **2**

PREP: **10 MINUTES**

(*SUPERMALT IF YOU'RE NOT ON A WAVE)

440ml can Guinness

100ml condensed milk

150ml whole milk

pinch of grated nutmeg

pinch of ground cinnamon

½ tsp vanilla bean paste

ice cubes

whipped cream, to serve

2 cinnamon sticks, to garnish

Classic yard man drink. You can respect the shop if they have good Guinness punch, but if you don't drink alcohol you can use Supermalt. Guinness punch is also a provider of the length and strength.

Whisk the Guinness, condensed milk, milk, spices and vanilla bean paste together in a jug. Pour into 2 glasses over ice cubes, then top with whipped cream and garnish with a cinnamon stick.

TEQUILA PINEAPPLE SLUSHY

SERVES: **2**

PREP: **10 MINUTES**

300g fresh diced pineapple, frozen, or ready-frozen pineapple

4 ice cubes

50ml tequila

juice of 2 limes, plus extra slices, to garnish

2 green jalapeños

80ml pineapple juice

½ tsp caster sugar

½ tsp chilli powder

pinch of salt

Do you wanna get waved but also cool off? This one will create a vibe and also complement any Mexican dish. Arriba! And if you're not on a drinking ting, just don't put in the tequila.

In a blender, blitz the frozen pineapple, ice, tequila, half the lime juice, 1 jalapeño and the pineapple juice to make a thick frozen drink.

Combine the sugar, chilli powder and salt on a plate. Put the remaining lime juice on another plate. Dip the rims of the chilled glasses into the lime juice followed by the chilli sugar. Pour the slushy into the glasses and serve garnished with a slice of lime and a jalapeño slice.

VOSSY, LEMONADE 'N' COLA

SERVES: **1**

PREP: **5 MINUTES**

25ml Courvoisier or other cognac

50ml lemonade

50ml cola

ice cubes

lime slices, to garnish

The only way to drink Vossy unless it's in the Big Zuu Bissap. The sweet flavours of the lemonade mix with the nice undertones of caramel from the cola. A couple of glasses of this, you'll be singing _Isn't She Lovely_ to a tree. Hang tight, Stevie Wonder.

Combine the liquid ingredients in a glass with plenty of ice cubes and serve, garnished with a slice of lime.

INDEX

ACKNOWLEDGEMENTS

Big up all my FAMILY *BackRoad Gee voice*

—

Isatu Hamzie, Mum ❤

Tubsey

Hyder

Ali Katal and his mum

Tubsey's mum

Hyder's mum and dad

Saskia and her mum (my Spanish babes)

The whole of the *Big Eats* crew

Boom, TwoFour and UKTV

BBC Books

The comedians and celebs we cooked for in *Big Eats*

Rosie for cooking the food

All the home ecs who made the dishes

Alex and Ro for coming up with half of 'em

Mark Wiens, the G.O.A.T.

AJ and JME for their recipes

The fans for supporting me

Liverpool FC, just because

Mo Salah for the Mo Salad

My lil brother Feroz, for being a G

My managers Matt and Georgie

Sierra Leone and Lebanon for their dishes

Iraq and Kurdistan for making Tubsey and Hyder

God for making life and food

Gordon Ramsay, who inspired me to be a TV chef